DISEASE
IN HISTORY

Bruno Leone

DISEASE
IN HISTORY

Bruno Leone

ReferencePoint
Press®

San Diego, CA

For more information, contact:
ReferencePoint Press, Inc.
PO Box 27779
San Diego, CA 92198
www. ReferencePointPress.com

LIBRARY OF CONGRESS CATALOGING-IN-PUBLICATION DATA

Leone, Bruno, 1939-
  Disease in history / by Bruno Leone.
    pages cm
  Audience: Grades 9 to 12.
  Includes bibliographical references and index.
   ISBN 978-1-60152-960-2 (hardback) -- ISBN 1-60152-960-0 (hardback) 1. Communicable diseases--History--Juvenile literature. 2. Communicable diseases--Social aspects--History--Juvenile literature. 3. Plague--Europe--History--Juvenile literature. 4. Plague--Social aspects--Europe--History--Juvenile literature. I. Title.
  RA643.L457 2016
  362.1969--dc23
                                                                    2015036750

CONTENTS

IMPORTANT EVENTS IN THE HISTORY OF DISEASE

430 BCE
Typhus epidemic breaks out in the city-state of Athens. Athens loses its war with Sparta.

165 CE
Lucius Verus, Marcus Aurelius's adoptive brother and coemperor, dies in Rome during a smallpox epidemic.

542
The bubonic plague, which occurred during the reign of the eastern emperor Justinian I, ends all hopes of reuniting the Roman Empire.

1879
Louis Pasteur develops a vaccine to prevent anthrax.

250   500   1000   1500

250
The Plague of Cyprian kills tens of thousands as Rome's borders begin to weaken.

476
Its population depleted by disease and warfare, the Western Roman Empire falls.

1665
The bubonic plague unleashes its final major assault upon Europe with the Great Plague of London.

1674
Using his microscope, Antoni van Leeuwenhoek discovers what he terms *animalcules* (germs).

1348
The second bout of bubonic plague hits western Europe and keeps surfacing for three hundred years.

6

1983
Doctors at the Pasteur Institute in France report they have isolated HIV, the virus responsible for AIDS.

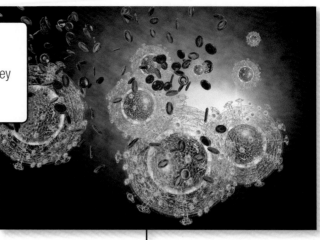

1905
Robert Koch wins the Nobel Prize in Medicine for identifying the bacillus responsible for tuberculosis.

2015
To date, 40 million people have died of AIDS-related illnesses.

1967
US surgeon general William H. Stewart announces that the war against infectious diseases has been won; history proves him wrong.

1900   1930   1960   1990

1928
Alexander Fleming discovers penicillin; in 1945 he receives a Nobel Prize for this work.

1955
Jonas Salk's polio vaccine is introduced.

2014
Outbreak of the largest Ebola epidemic in history sickens and kills thousands of people in West Africa.

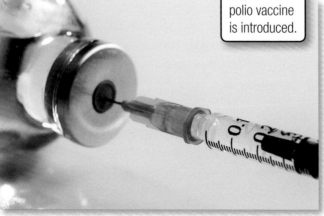

INTRODUCTION

The Importance of Disease in History

Famed psychiatrist Carl Jung once exclaimed, "Man has come to be man's worst enemy."[1] When he uttered those words, Jung was referring to humanity's propensity for warfare and the horrific consequences war may one day generate in an age of nuclear weapons. Ever since the dawn of world civilization in the ancient Near East, armed conflict has played an unquestionable and frequent role in the death of people, the destruction of nations, and the shattering of the human mind and spirit. Historians Will and Ariel Durant note in their book *The Lessons of History* that "in the last 3,421 years of recorded history only 268 have seen no war."[2]

Yet in reality, another enemy is lurking beyond the boundaries of warfare—an enemy which in almost every respect is more grim, pervasive, menacing, and invasive than armed conflict has been thus far. Indeed, it repeatedly surpasses war in the number of casualties it claims. Moreover, unlike war, this enemy awaits mindless and unseen, wreaking its havoc while unaware of moral concepts like mercy and peace and totally without fear of reprisal. And although visually unnoticed, it openly resides in all corners and habitats of the planet Earth, constituting nearly twenty-five times the total biomass of all animal life. In a word, it is virtually omnipresent. This adversary of humankind is collectively referred to as microorganisms, microbes, or—most commonly—germs.

It is remarkable, however, that despite their numbers and prevalence, the overwhelming majority of microbes inhabiting the planet are harmless. Indeed, many make distinctively positive contributions to the environment and to the well-being of the human organism. For instance, a significant number of soil-dwelling microbes are responsible for decomposing the ground they occupy and in so doing create nitrates necessary for plant growth. Furthermore, there are microorganisms that inhabit the human intestinal tract and whose colonies collectively total over 100 trillion organisms. Sometimes referred to as gut flora, these species play an essential and beneficial part in aiding in the digestion and eventual elimination of food consumed by their human host.

Disease-Bearing Microbes

Unfortunately, a highly effective minority of microbes do trigger varying degrees of illness in Earth's human and nonhuman animal populations. The numbers of microbial species represented by this minority are clearly disproportionate to the impact they sometimes wield upon the health and well-being of the hosts they inhabit. They can be responsible for conditions ranging from the common cold, which passes in almost all cases in one to two weeks and usually requires no medical treatment, to conditions like rabies, which, if untreated, is almost always terminal. Furthermore, they are also accountable for epidemic disorders such as influenza, bubonic plague, smallpox, and cholera, which, at varying periods in history, have been responsible for an extraordinarily high number of fatalities—at times well into the tens of millions.

Almost all disease-bearing microbes appear to have one thing in common: they are opportunistic. That is, they enter and thrive in their human hosts whenever the opportunity presents itself. Many are long-term occupants in or on the human body and stand ready to attack with the force and stealth of an invading army whenever they encounter weaknesses in the body's defense systems. Once established, they multiply, develop into colonies, and weaken their host organism to a greater or lesser degree depending upon their numbers and virulence.

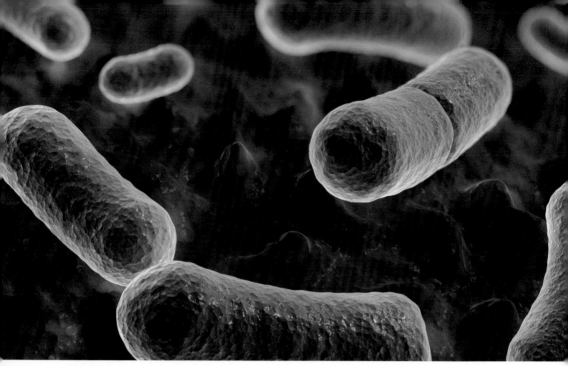

Yersinia pestis *(pictured)* is the bacterium responsible for bubonic plague. Disease-carrying microbes such as this have killed tens of millions of people throughout recorded history.

Research and the Historical Record

There is a broad range of disagreement as to the total number of helpful, harmful, and harmless microbial species inhabiting Earth's land, sea, and air. Estimates range from hundreds of thousands to millions. The reason for this great disparity is generally twofold. First, scientists frequently differ over what characterizes a species or specific classification of microorganism. The determination of a species is based upon genetic similarities. Since microbes undergo frequent mutation or genetic alteration, it therefore is difficult at times to pinpoint the precise relationship between or among species. Second, locating and identifying different microbes can be complex and extremely costly. Ferreting out specific organisms, whether within or outside of the human body, can involve an expensive and formidable amount of equipment, research, and personnel. Historically, government and industry do not release funds for such projects with either ease or frequency.

When investigating the history of disease, historians and medical specialists regularly find it difficult to determine what organisms were responsible for specific epidemics that have occurred at decisive moments in history. Consequently, much of what is published on the topic of widespread diseases throughout history has required a broad spectrum of educated guesswork in the search for a diagnosis. The reason is that while the historical records being studied by contemporary researchers may contain a surplus of telltale signs like raging fevers, delirium, skin eruptions, nausea, vomiting, and others, symptoms such as these are shared by numerous diseases infecting humans and even other animals. Moreover, authors from the past who left written records of diseases and epidemics they either witnessed or heard of secondhand often were writing at times and in places where medical knowledge was woefully inadequate or even nonexistent. It therefore becomes the responsibility of the historian to make the diagnosis with no laboratory or diagnostic tools other than the written account of medically untrained individuals who lived centuries or millennia ago.

Diseases Shape History

It was not until the nineteenth and twentieth centuries that sophisticated, thorough, and accurate methods for diagnosing diseases began to develop. Along with advanced diagnostic techniques and equipment, modern governments and private health-related agencies are now utilizing more comprehensive methods and systems to record incidents, monitor causes, and ensure control of outbreaks of local or epidemic diseases.

But throughout history one fact can be credibly argued: disease has been, and to date remains, humankind's greatest and most dangerous villain and at times has significantly influenced the twists and turns taken by history. Scientist and author Jared Diamond underscores this assertion in his Pulitzer Prize–winning book, *Guns, Germs, and Steel: The Fates of Human Societies.* "The major killers of humanity throughout history," he writes, "are infectious diseases. . . . Because diseases have been the biggest killers of people, they have also been decisive shapers of history."[3]

CHAPTER ONE

Do Infectious Diseases Impact upon History?

For diseases to reach epidemic proportions and become, as Jared Diamond noted, "decisive shapers of history," a virulent and communicable microorganism must be involved. Not all diseases are caused by contagious microbes. Diabetes and most cardiac disorders, for example, are attributed to many different factors, including genetics and lifestyle choices such as improper diet and lack of exercise. Degeneration of the macula of the eye—which can eventually lead to blindness—is usually part of the aging process with accompanying factors such as smoking and chronic obesity placing people at greater risk for contracting the disease. Contact with individuals who suffer from the above-mentioned conditions, along with a large number of other illnesses, would be a threat to no one.

An infectious disease—as opposed to an inherited one— almost always is transmissible, provided that a microorganism is available to be transferred to a susceptible host. Such a microbe can then spread from carrier to carrier by either direct contact (an infected carrier sneezes or coughs, spraying a nearby person) or indirect contact (a hand swarming with infectious microbes touches a doorknob that is later touched by an unknowing victim). Depending upon how many people are infected, the disease can be classified as *endemic* (restricted or distinctive to a locality or region and having a low mortality rate), *epidemic* (affecting a large number of people within a specific community or region), or *pandemic* (covering a wide geographic area and affecting a very high proportion of the population). The contagion can be one of several generic categories of microscopic organisms, each of which is potentially harmful and even deadly to human and non-human animals. The most common types of contagions are fungi, viruses, bacteria, and protozoa. And of these, viruses and bacteria have been by far the most recurrent and have had the most extensive impact upon human events. An epidemic that struck the city of Athens, Greece, in 430 BCE illustrates the effects of highly virulent and contagious microorganisms upon humans and ultimately upon history. As University of Edinburgh medical microbiology professor Dorothy H. Crawford notes, this particular epidemic, the so-called Plague of Athens, "is the oldest epidemic ever recorded [and] documented by [a] contemporary historian, Thucydides."[4]

Athens: The Glory of Ancient Greece

Ancient Greece was a loosely knit confederation of city-states, each referred to as a polis. The Greek city-states, or poleis, while for the most part sharing a common heritage, were politically independent and at times competed economically and even militarily. However, the poleis were also known to unite in the face of a common enemy, such as when the Persian Empire, under its dynamic king Darius I the Great, invaded Greece in 492 BCE. Due in large part to the city-state of Athens, whose combined army and navy were the most effective in the Greek military, Persia was soundly defeated nearly fifteen years later.

Unquestionably, Athens surpassed each of the Greek poleis in virtually all respects. Athens stood at the forefront of ancient Greece's golden age. Attica, the territory surrounding and controlled by Athens, was large and rich in natural resources such as marble for building and metals for coins and weapons. Athens itself enjoyed the advantage of an excellent natural water supply and was protected by four mountain ranges. Nature also favored

13

Attica with a long coastline that supported Athens's maritime interests. Not only did Athens possess an effective army and a superior navy, but it also was held in legendary esteem as being the birthplace of democracy. Finally, its celebrated cultural achievements in philosophy, literature, architecture, and science were matchless in the ancient world. When historians write of the glory that was Greece, it is primarily in the direction of ancient Athens that they are looking.

Well aware of its own preeminence, Athens kept striving to dominate greater Greece. Following the war with Persia, Athens was instrumental in forming the Delian League, a union of most of

Around 430 BCE sailors arriving in the port city of Piraeus (pictured) unknowingly spread a contagion that would have dire consequences for Athens. Nearly one-third of those who contracted the illness died.

the city-states whose purpose was the defense of Greece. Controlled by Athens, the league provided the seed for what shortly blossomed into the Athenian empire. However, when Athens began demanding tribute from league members, the polis of Sparta rebelled. With the backing of its powerful army, Sparta allied with several other city-states and launched an attack against the Athenians. The result was the Peloponnesian War, a conflict that lasted twenty-seven years (431–404 BCE), with Sparta and Athens the primary combatants.

Before wide-scale hostilities began, Pericles, the renowned statesman and head of the Athenian government, convinced his fellow citizens to adopt a defensive strategy in order to avoid direct combat with the Spartan army. The plan called for all citizens, military and civilian (including rural inhabitants), to be brought into the city where they would be safe behind the reinforced city walls. Athens would then rely upon its powerful navy to supply its citizens with necessary food and sundries while the entire Athenian military would steadily wear down the forces of Sparta and her allies. Although the plan was strategically sound, it could not anticipate an event that would render it a colossal failure and prove to be one of the major contributions to the defeat of Athens in the Peloponnesian War.

Contagion Spreads Across the Sea

In the year 430 BCE an epidemic originating in Ethiopia and passing through the seaports of Egypt and Libya made its way eastward across the Mediterranean Sea on cargo ships manned by infected sailors. The epidemic eventually entered Athens through the port city of Piraeus. The severely overcrowded conditions in the city, a consequence of the newly instituted military plan of Pericles, contributed to the epidemic's rapid spread. The result was that eventually most of the inhabitants of Athens became infected and nearly one-third of those (both military and civilian) died in due course. The high mortality rate reflected the fact that science and medicine in Greece at the time of the plague was still in its early stages. Any attempts by contemporary Athenian physicians to either diagnosis or prescribe a rational and effective treatment for victims of the epidemic was beyond the realm of their knowledge and experience.

The most valuable historical source for the Plague of Athens was the Greek general Thucydides. An Athenian, Thucydides wrote *The History of the Peloponnesian War,* which the authoritative *Oxford Companion to Classical Literature* labeled "one of the greatest historical works of all time, notable for its condensed, direct, and graphic style, for its fairness and scientific method . . . and for its reasoning on political questions."[5] Thucydides's account of the symptoms and mortality rate of the plague is comprehensive and apparently accurate enough to provide historians and modern diagnostic experts with sufficient information to develop informed though cautious diagnoses. Will Durant, for example, describes the event as "a plague—probably malaria—which raged for nearly three years, killing a fourth of the soldiers and a great number of the civilian population."[6] Frederick F. Cartwright, Emeritus Senior Lecturer in the History of Medicine, University of London, claims that "the majority opinion holds that this was a highly malignant form of scarlet fever." He continues, however, conceding that "other authorities have suggested bubonic plague, typhus, smallpox, measles, and anthrax of unusual virulence."[7]

The University of Maryland School of Medicine's Historical Clinicopathological Conference focused its 1999 annual meeting upon the Plague of Athens. Dr. David Durack, a consulting professor of medicine at Duke University, where he had been chief of the Division of Infectious Diseases, headed a team of medical detectives attempting to determine the nature of the epidemic. Durack concluded, "Epidemic typhus fever is the best explanation. It hits hardest in times of war and privation. . . . It kills the victim after about seven days, and it sometimes causes a striking complication: gangrene of the tips of the fingers and toes. The Plague of Athens had all these features."[8]

Problems Identifying Historical Epidemics

Hans Zinsser was a highly regarded physician, author, and Harvard biologist. His book *Rats, Lice, and History* is one of the first books ever written that deals with the influence disease has had upon history. Throughout the book, Zinsser emphasizes that most major epidemics recorded in history are worsened by other, accompanying contagious diseases.

> The oldest recorded epidemic often regarded as an outbreak of typhus is the Athenian plague of the Peloponnesian Wars, which is described in the Second Book of the History of Thucydides. In trying to make the diagnosis of epidemics from ancient descriptions . . . it is important to remember that in any great outbreak, while the large majority of cases may represent a single type of infection, there is usually . . . [an] increase in other forms of contagious diseases. . . . Very rarely is there a pure epidemic of a single malady. It is [likely] that the description of Thucydides is confused by the fact that a number of diseases were epidemic in Athens at the time of the great plague. The conditions were ripe for it. [However,] the plague of Athens, whatever it may have been, had a profound effect upon historical events.

Hans Zinsser, *Rats, Lice, and History*. New York: Bantam, 1967, pp. 87–88.

Thucydides's account of the symptoms, mortality rate, and other facets of the plague seem to favor Durack's diagnosis but does not necessarily exclude other possibilities. (Durack himself felt compelled to admit that "the Plague of Athens . . . has fascinated doctors and historians for centuries . . . [even] if we can never be absolutely sure what caused the plague."[9])

In History of the Peloponnesian War, *the Greek general Thucydides (pictured) provided invaluable descriptions of the Plague of Athens. His account includes his own experiences as someone who contracted the disease and survived.*

Moreover, Thucydides's narrative carries with it the firsthand knowledge of a man who himself was a victim of the plague and survived. As he notes in the opening section of his history, "I shall describe [the plague's] actual course, explaining the symptoms, from the study of which a person should be best

18

able, having knowledge of it beforehand, to recognize it if it should ever break out again. For I had the disease myself and saw others sick of it."[10]

Ravaged by a Plague

Thucydides provides a lucid and coherent explanation of the plague—its uniqueness, high death rate, and the degree to which physicians were not only baffled but also fell victim to it:

> A similar disorder is said to have previously smitten many places, particularly Lemnos [an island in the Aegean Sea], but there is no record of such a pestilence occurring elsewhere, or of so great a destruction of human life. For a while physicians, in ignorance of the nature of the disease, sought to apply remedies; but it was in vain, and they themselves were among the first victims, because they oftenest came into contact with it. No human art was of any avail and as to [prayers] in temples . . . they were utterly useless.[11]

The Athenian general-turned-historian then proceeds to describe the onset and symptoms of the epidemic: "It struck the healthy without warning, starting with high fever in the head, and a reddening and inflammation of the eyes. Internally, the throat and tongue became immediately inflamed, and the breath was labored and foul." The initial symptoms included fits of sneezing and sore throats. This was followed in a short while by an almost incessant cough as the condition began moving downward into the chest. When it entered the area of the stomach, it produced acute indigestion and vomiting of bile. These abdominal symptoms were accompanied by severe pain and unproductive retching. The patient's exterior was red and full of blemishes that would erupt into sores and small boil-like pustules. Thucydides points out that the victims developed extremely high fevers so that they "could not stand even the lightest clothes of muslin being thrown on them. They much preferred to lie quite naked." Thucydides explains how, suggestive of typhus fever, "the disease started in the head and spread downwards through the whole body. If anyone survived the first attacks he still was marked by the loss of his extremities, for it attacked the genitals and the tips of the hands and feet. Many lost these, or even their eyes, and lived."[12]

The crowded conditions in the city severely intensified the plague's impact upon the Athenians. Thucydides notes that transferring thousands of "people out of the country into the city aggravated the misery. . . . The newly arrived suffered most. For, having no houses of their own, but inhabiting in the height of summer stifling huts, the mortality among them was dreadful, and they perished in wild disorder. The dead lay as they had died one upon another." Finally, Thucydides portrays what can only be described as an alarmed and disheartened population:

> The temples in which [the people] lodged were full of corpses of those who died in them; for the violence of the calamity was such that men, not knowing where to turn, grew reckless of all law, human and divine. . . . Those who saw all perishing alike, thought that the worship or neglect of the Gods made no difference. For offences against human law no punishment was to be feared; no one would live long enough to be called to account. . . . Such was the grievous calamity which now afflicted the Athenians; within the walls their people were dying, and without, their country was being ravaged.[13]

Typhus: A Deadly Pestilence

Epidemic typhus has been one of the most common and deadly pestilences humankind has faced since the rise of cities and litera-

One of History's Deadliest Killers

Mary Dobson is a research associate for the Department of History and Philosophy of Science at the University of Cambridge in England. An expert in the history of infectious diseases and the relationship between disease and environment, she presents below a brief overview of one of history's deadliest killers, typhus:

> Typhus is an acute infectious disease that is transmitted by *Pediculus humanus corporis* — or, as is more commonly known, the body louse. For centuries typhus was especially prevalent where there was overcrowding and poor standards of hygiene, causing horrible suffering and innumerable deaths. There are many graphic descriptions of epidemics during wars and famines, and on a number of occasions the disease has even changed the course of human history. However, by the end of the Second World War a combination of vaccination, insecticides and antibiotics had led to a decline in the incidence of typhus. It is now relatively uncommon, but does still occur in parts of Asia, Africa and central and South America.

Mary Dobson, *Disease: The Extraordinary Stories Behind History's Deadliest Killers*. London: Quercus, 2007, p. 36.

cy and perhaps even before the rise of civilizations. It becomes rife during times of warfare and famine, both of which have plagued society for several millennia and each of which tend to nurture conditions under which the disease can arise and flourish with relative ease. There are specific situations that are known to contribute to outbreaks of typhus. These include overcrowded living conditions; decline in agricultural production due to insect infestation; drought or worker shortages during wartime; close proximity of healthy and diseased persons; overall decline in sanitation and health awareness; prison, concentration, and refugee camps congested with inmates; and other similar situations. During the last two centuries, for example, there have been several particularly virulent outbreaks of the disease. The deadliest have occurred during the Napoleonic Wars, the Irish Potato Famine, the Crimean War, and World Wars I and II. In fact, immediately following World War I over 5 million Russian and eastern Europeans alone died of typhus.

Epidemic typhus is caused by a type of bacteria called *Rickettsia prowazekii*. The bacteria are carried by vectors, or intermediaries, known as lice (singular: louse), parasitic insects that live on the skin of their hosts. In humans, the primary vector is the body louse. A louse becomes infected when it bites and sucks in the blood of an infected person, ingesting the bacteria as it does so. Once the bacteria have entered the louse's gut, they will keep multiplying until they have invaded the entire intestinal tract. The disease then spreads to others as the body louse moves to a different host carrying its deadly cargo of rickettsia with it. Each new host becomes a potential victim as the contents of the louse's bacteria-filled intestinal canal is passed onto the skin of the host whenever the louse defecates.

The transmission process itself is fairly simple and can occur in several ways. Humans become infected when they scratch the bite area, which is usually covered with lice feces crawling with rickettsia. Scratching generally causes the skin to break, thereby allowing the bacteria to enter the host's bloodstream. (The bacteria will retain its viability for several days, even in dried louse feces). An infected louse also can cause the spread of typhus when it bites and attempts to draw blood from its victim. Since the rickettsia contained in its gut usually will be present in the louse's saliva, the bacteria are able to enter the host's bloodstream and infect it. Finally, dead infected lice and the feces they leave behind will infest the clothing of their human prey. Since the bacteria generally outlive the lice, they easily can be transmitted to persons who come in direct contract with the contaminated clothing.

A body louse feeds on a human host. Lice (the plural of louse) carry the bacteria that cause typhus, a disease that has devastated human populations at many points in history.

The mortality rate of epidemic typhus varies depending upon hygienic conditions, the degree of overcrowding, and the availability of food in the affected geographical areas. During the disease's later stages, the circulatory system frequently slows down. As a result, blood flow to the extremities diminishes, causing gangrene of the hands, feet, and genitals, with a subsequent loss of those parts of the body (as noted in Thucydides's account). The direct cause of death for typhus is generally kidney or heart failure. Untreated (as was primarily the case in Athens), the death rate may reach as high as 30 to 35 percent.

Typhus Contributes to the Downfall of Athens
Many historians agree that whatever its cause (typhus, smallpox, scarlet fever, measles, malaria, bubonic plague, or any

combination of those), the plague contributed not only to the defeat of Athens during the Peloponnesian War—more than two decades after the war's onset—but ultimately to the decline of ancient Greek civilization as well. In her book *Deadly Companions: How Microbes Shaped Our History*, Dorothy H. Crawford writes that "when the epidemic struck in 430 BC it was so virulent and widespread that it spelt defeat for the Athenians, thus contributing to the end of the golden age of Greek culture and their dominance of the ancient world."[14] Medical

The navies of Athens and Sparta battle at sea during the Peloponnesian War. A deadly epidemic contributed to the defeat of Athens—and the eventual decline of ancient Greek civilization.

historian Cartwright unequivocally states, "The plague of Athens undoubtedly contributed to the downfall of the Athenian empire. By killing so large a number, by demoralizing the capital and, above all, by destroying the fighting power of the navy, the plague prevented Athens striking a decisive blow at Sparta. The war dragged on for twenty-seven years and ended with the defeat of Athens in 404 B.C."[15]

Pericles himself, Athens's brilliant leader, died of the plague in 429 BCE, but not before the distraught statesman saw his wife and two sons fall victim to it. Unable to find leadership comparable to Pericles and with the death of so many of its able-bodied citizens, Athens wafted like a rudderless ship from one misfortune to another. When the Peloponnesian War began, Athens had anticipated and seemed assured of a relatively swift victory. The opposite proved true. As historian Edward McNall Burns notes, because of the plague

> [Athens's] trade was destroyed, her democracy overthrown, and her population decimated. . . . Quite as bad was the moral degradation which followed in the wake of the military reverses. . . . Ultimately, deserted by all her allies except Samos [a Greek island in the eastern Aegean Sea] and with her food supply cut off, Athens was left with no alternative but to surrender or starve.[16]

Historians generally avoid stating the obvious, such as how different history may have been, had a pivotal historical event not occurred. However, award-winning writer and history professor William H. McNeill could not resist the temptation. In his much-acclaimed book *Plagues and Peoples,* he writes that "the [plague] inflicted a blow on Athenian society from which it never entirely recovered. This unforeseen and unforeseeable epidemiological accident . . . may have had much to do with the failure of Athenian plans for the defeat of Sparta and [its allies].

Had Athens won that war, how different the subsequent political history of the Mediterranean would have been!"[17]

Although the leadership of Athens was restored for a time during the fourth century BCE, for several reasons the recovery was short-lived. For one, the economic and political problems brought on by the prolonged and destructive war had taken a lasting toll on Athens and the city-state governmental system of ancient Greece. For another, Persia, Greece's traditional enemy, contributed to Athenian difficulties by regularly infusing rival Sparta and its allies with military and other strategic aid. But of greater import, Greece's neighbor to the north, the kingdom of Macedonia, was committed to territorial expansion. Under the able leadership of its king, Philip II (382–336 BCE), Macedonia embarked upon and succeeded in conquering nearly the whole of Greece before Philip's death. And Philip's storied son, Alexander the Great (356–323 BCE), not only completed his father's conquest of Greece but also extended the Macedonian Empire westward to Egypt and eastward to India.

CHAPTER TWO

Plague and the Fall of the Roman Empire

Alexander the Great of Macedonia was not only a conqueror but also a visionary. Under the influence of his teacher, the famed philosopher/scientist Aristotle, he foresaw a world where all of the lands he had conquered, as well as those he hoped yet to conquer, would unite under a common banner. Such a world, he believed, was destined to usher in an era of peace and prosperity for all peoples residing there. Had he realized his final dream, he would have been instrumental in influencing the geopolitical history of the Middle East and Asia for many centuries to come. Instead, the Macedonian king died unexpectedly and prematurely after suffering a high fever for ten days. As historian Edward Mc-Nall Burns emphasizes, "The death of Alexander the Great in 323 B.C. constituted a watershed in the development of world history. Hellenic [Greek] civilization as it had existed in its prime now came to an end."[18] Many historians have speculated that Alexander's premature death (he died one month short of his thirty-third birthday) resulted either from typhoid fever, measles, or malaria, each respectively caused by a bacterium, a virus, and a protozoan.

But beyond speculation is the fact that his death in 323 BCE created a power vacuum in the eastern Mediterranean. Having left no heirs or designated successors, Alexander's highest-ranking generals chose to divide his empire among themselves. Dissatisfied with the partition, the younger army officers challenged their superiors, giving rise to a series of wars that finally ended with no one commander or coalition force emerging victorious. The result of these conflicts was that the 2-million-square-mile (5.2-million-sq.-km) realm that Alexander had forged in his short lifetime was left divided and considerably weakened. As a consequence of this divisive political situation and lack of centralized authority, a shift occurred in the axis of power in the Mediterranean world. That change would ultimately favor the ascendency of a little-known city located on the Italian Peninsula approximately 650 miles (1,046 km) west of Athens. That city was Rome.

The Rise of Rome

Nestled on the banks of the Tiber River in west-central Italy and built upon seven hills, Rome was one of many city-states that spanned the entire Italian Peninsula. Historical sources for the early period in Roman history are scanty. Perhaps the best source, Roman historian Titus Livius, known as Livy (59 BCE–17 CE), noted that from the eighth to the sixth century BCE Rome was ruled by kings. In 509, however, the monarchy was overthrown in favor of a republican form of government. As a republic, executive authority resided in two elected officials called consuls who were voted into office annually by assemblies of Roman citizens. The most powerful and authoritative of the assemblies was the Roman senate, a legislative body dominated by patricians, or upper-class citizens. It was during the era of the republic that Rome began its rise to power in the western Mediterranean. Yet the history of the Roman Republic was a turbulent one characterized by political unrest at home and nearly continual warfare abroad. The domestic disagreements resulted from the plebeians, or lower-class citizens, agitating for and incrementally being granted more and more power by the aristocratic senate. And the persistent flood of foreign wars that accompanied the internal

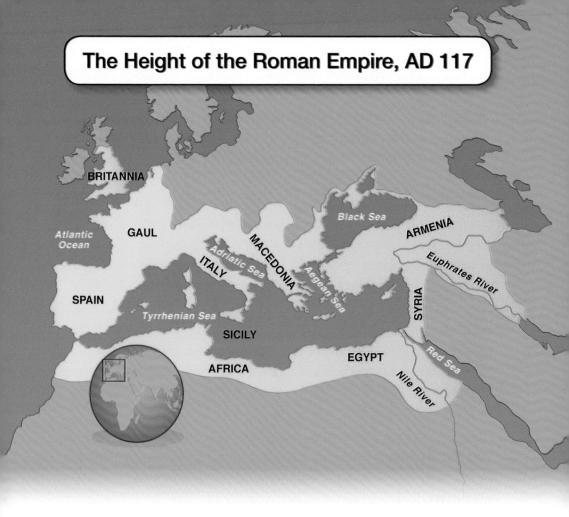

The Height of the Roman Empire, AD 117

BRITANNIA

Atlantic
Ocean

GAUL

SPAIN

ITALY

Adriatic Sea

Tyrrhenian Sea

MACEDONIA

Aegean Sea

Black Sea

ARMENIA

Euphrates River

SYRIA

SICILY

AFRICA

EGYPT

Red Sea

Nile River

strife was driven by a chauvinistic conviction that Rome's destiny was to rule the Mediterranean world.

The Romans were remarkably successful in achieving their goal of supremacy throughout the Mediterranean and beyond. Within 250 years of establishing the republic, this deceptively ordinary city-state on the Tiber River managed to acquire political power over virtually the whole Italian Peninsula. Moreover, during the next quarter of a millennium, Rome gained control of the entire coastlines of both the eastern and western Mediterranean. Before the beginning of the Common Era, however, a series of civil wars succeeded in bringing the republican government to an end in 27 BCE, during which year it was replaced by the *principate,* or "empire." While the consuls, senate, and other legislative bodies remained a part of the new government, absolute power now resided in the hands of the *princeps,* or "emperor," also known by the titles *caesar* and *augustus*.

It was in the second century, during the reign of the emperor Trajan (98–117), that Roman power reached its zenith. The period is often referred to as Rome's golden age or the era of the Five Good Emperors (Nerva, Trajan, Hadrian, Antoninus Pius, and Marcus Aurelius). At that time, the empire covered slightly less than 2.5 million square miles (6.5 million sq km)—nearly comparable in size to the continental United States. Territorially, it included the entire Mediterranean Sea (which Romans referred to as *Mare Nostrum*, "Our Sea"); areas as far east as the Black Sea, Armenia, and Azerbaijan; the entire northern coast of Africa; and much of what today is considered western Europe, including most of Britain. Furthermore, Rome's legions were stationed throughout this vast empire and charged with maintaining peace and order, a duty at which they largely excelled. The legions essentially were utilized as fortresses of troops strategically located on the empire's borders (yet mobile) to prevent both peaceful and military violations of Rome's territorial sovereignty. The system worked so well that historians refer to the first two centuries of the empire as the Pax Romana, or "Roman Peace." Not before or since in human history have there been two hundred consecutive years of relative peace on so wide a geographical scale. No nation seriously challenged the might of Rome as its foreign policy continued to reflect the venerated Latin proverb *Si vis pacem, para bellum*—"If you want peace, be prepared for war" (similar to the modern maxims "Peace through strength" and "The best offense is a good defense"). Indeed, if a single word can be found that best describes Rome during its golden age, that word would be *invincible*.

Disease Travels with the Roman Legions

But microbes do not fear armies and are unmindful of proverbs. And even more ominously, they not only prey on military personnel but also exploit them as carriers. In truth, armies historically are one of the most effective agents in the transmission of microscopic pathogens between cities and across continents. Even Rome (or *especially* Rome, with its legions stationed throughout its vast empire) at the height of its power and invincibility was not immune to microbial invasions.

Throughout its history, Rome, like all ancient cities and countries, was subject to epidemics of varying degrees. Outbreaks of infectious diseases date back to the Roman Republic. William H. McNeill notes that the Roman historian Livy "records at least eleven cases of pestilential disaster in republican times, the earliest dated 387 B.C. Another epidemic of considerable measure struck the city of Rome in A.D. 65 [during the reign of the emperor Nero]." However, McNeill then emphasizes that these earlier epidemics "paled before the disease that began spreading through the Roman empire in A.D. 165."[19]

The plague of 165 began during the reign of the emperor Marcus Aurelius. Usually referred to as the Antonine Plague after the dynasty into which the emperor was adopted, the plague was transmitted throughout the empire by Roman legions that had been sent to Mesopotamia (modern Iraq) to shore up Rome's southeastern borders. According to classical scholar David Potter, as the troops were withdrawing, "a sudden and devastating natural disaster [occurred]. A pandemic illness took hold in Mesopotamia while the Romans were mopping up there. As they returned to their posts around the empire, the legions brought the disease with them."[20]

Contemporary historical sources for the plague are sparse. Yet despite that, it is still reasonably apparent that the number of victims was exceedingly high. For one thing, evidence reveals that the disease spread throughout the *entire* empire and eventually into India and China. Moreover, it lasted several decades, tapering off into the third century, more than forty years after it began. In some areas of the empire, as many as half of those infected died of the disease. The total number of deaths

The Antonine Plague Weakens Rome's Defenses

The Antonine Plague created the first breach in Rome's frontier defenses. Beginning in 165, it took its annual toll not only within the Roman army itself but also among the German tribes attempting to fight their way across Rome's borders. Frederick F. Cartwright, Emeritus Senior Lecturer in the History of Medicine, University of London, identified the disease as smallpox.

> The pestilence raged until A.D. 180; one of the last victims was the noblest of Roman emperors, Marcus Aurelius. He died on the seventh day of his illness and is said to have refused to see his son at the last, fearing lest he, too should succumb. After A.D. 180 there came a short respite followed by a return in 189. The spread of this second epidemic seems to have been less wide, but mortality in Rome was ghastly; as many as 2,000 died in a single day. . . . There is . . . some semblance to the Athenian plague, but the undoubted Eastern origin and the mention of pustules have led many historians to assert that this was the first instance of a smallpox epidemic.

Frederick F. Cartwright, *Disease and History*. New York: New American Library, 1974, pp. 19–20.

is estimated to run as high as 5 million. And like all plagues, this one did not discriminate, drawing its victims from all levels of society—old and young, rich and poor, freeman and slave. Lucius Verus, Marcus Aurelius's adoptive brother and coemperor, was one of the plague's earliest victims.

The Romans had no cure or treatment for the disease. Galen, the famous Greek physician who was residing in Rome at the court of Marcus Aurelius when the plague began, described it as a fever plague. Drawing from Galen's observations, microbiologist Dorothy H. Crawford notes that the plague's symptoms included

> intense heat and thirst, vomiting and diarrhea, all very simi-
> lar to the plague of Athens, but this time there is a clear de-
> scription of a dry, black, ulcerated rash covering the whole
> body, which Galen attributes to "a remnant of blood which
> had putrefied in the fever blisters." This description, par-
> ticularly of the rash, leaves little doubt that the plague was
> smallpox, possibly the first of its kind in Europe.

Crawford then writes that "some experts still favour typhus as the cause, maintaining that in its early stages it cannot be distinguished from smallpox."[21]

Given the large number of victims, however, a diagnosis of smallpox seems more likely. A high mortality rate—as was the case with the Antonine Plague—is a telling sign that immunity is very low or totally absent in a given population. Such an absence of immunity often indicates that a contagion is making its initial appearance. Immunity to widespread diseases generally is found in areas previously infected by a given pathogen; as a result, antibodies have amassed in the population, enabling many to fight off later outbreaks of the disease.

A Second Plague Ravages Rome

Despite the enormous death toll of the Antonine Plague, the empire managed to endure and eventually might have recovered much of its former strength. However, two occurrences in the third century made the possibility of recovery exceedingly difficult. The first was political in nature and involved the instability of the imperial office of emperor. Between the years 235 and 284, twenty-six different emperors ruled, but only one died a natural death. During those years, army officers and government officials, along with their cadre of loyal followers, were continually vying for the emperorship and were willing to employ assassination as a means to obtain it. The lone third-century emperor who managed to restore any semblance of order and power in Rome was Diocletian, a cavalry commander who was declared emperor by his troops in 284. But despite his achievements and with more left to accomplish, Diocletian chose to abdicate in 305. He retired to his palace in Split in modern Croatia, where he spent the rest of his life raising cabbages. He died in 311, one of the few remaining Roman emperors to experience a natural death before the Western Roman Empire fell during the fifth century.

Of greater consequence was a second plague that ravaged Rome less than a half century after the end of the Antonine Plague. Referred to as the Plague of Cyprian, it began in 250 and was named after the Christian bishop of Carthage, a city in North Africa exceptionally hard hit by the new epidemic. Pontius of Carthage, who was Cyprian's biographer, described the outbreak of the plague:

> There broke out a dreadful plague, and excessive destruction of a hateful disease invaded every house in succession of the trembling populace, carrying off day by day with abrupt attack numberless people, every one from his own house. All were shuddering, fleeing, shunning the contagion, impiously exposing their own friends, as if with the exclusion of the person who was sure to die of the plague, one could exclude death itself also. There lay about the meanwhile, over the whole city, no longer bodies, but the carcasses of many, and, by the contemplation of a lot which in their turn would be theirs, demanded the pity of the passers-by for themselves. No one regarded anything besides his cruel gains. No one trembled at the remembrance of a similar event.[22]

Cyprian himself kept a written tract of the plague that he called *De Mortalitate*. Referring specifically to Cyprian's account, author George C. Kohn notes that the bishop listed "the various symp-

Roman soldiers force their captives to march through the city. As the Roman legions conquered territories far and wide, they extended their empire's reach but also spread disease-carrying germs that resulted in a devastating plague.

toms of the disease, from the red eyes and inflamed throat that came first, to the gangrene of the feet and the continual vomiting and diarrhea that followed, and finally the loss of hearing and eyesight that afflicted many who recovered." Kohn also notes that according to other ancient writers, "most victims also suffered from burning fever and unquenchable thirst . . . [and] that the disease could be spread indirectly through the clothing of an infected person."[23] At its peak, the epidemic claimed five thousand lives a day in Rome itself. There is no agreement among historians and diagnosticians as to the nature of the disease, although many argue that it was a repeat of the smallpox epidemic. Others, however, have pointed out that the symptoms more closely match measles. Measles, an acute infectious disease, seems the likely culprit since it would have been new to the Mediterranean area, thereby explaining the lack of immunity and high death rate.

Rome Founders as Its Populace Succumbs to Disease

Whatever its cause, the Plague of Cyprian was a heavy blow to Rome, already embattled on many fronts. Layer upon layer of hardship had been afflicting the troubled empire during the third century. In addition to the shakiness of the imperial throne, barbarian tribes residing in Germania, just to the north and east of the empire (and virtually always a security issue), were now crossing its borders in increasing numbers and aggressiveness. The deteriorating situation presented Roman authorities with a difficult dilemma that the plague made nearly insoluble. While the latest plague was causing a serious reduction in Rome's population, concurrently, the invasions were creating a largely unanswered need for additional manpower to help bolster the beleaguered Roman legions. And the costs related to both plague and invasions gave rise to severe treasury shortages that in turn triggered escalating taxes and inflation, thereby creating economic problems at all levels of Roman society. Crawford emphasizes that the "plague caused such a calamitous drop in population that the Roman Empire, critically reliant on manpower for its every function, began to founder. Town and fields stood empty, the army was depleted, trade and commerce stagnated, and the people were confused and demoralized."[24]

The Dominant Influence of Plague

William H. McNeill is a distinguished historian and winner of the National Book Award in 1964 for his acclaimed *The Rise of the West*. In *Plagues and Peoples*, he offers a compelling explanation of the catastrophic socioeconomic effect disease exerted upon the Roman imperial system.

The Roman imperial system collected tax moneys from lands close to the sea and transferred spare cash to the armies stationed at the frontiers. This remained a viable arrangement . . . until the heavy blow of unfamiliar disease seriously eroded the wealth of the Mediterranean heartlands between A.D. 165 and 266. Thereupon, rapid die-off of large proportions of the urban populations at the most active centers of Mediterranean commerce diminished the flow of cash to the imperial [treasury]. . . . [Yet] the ravages of armies, and the ruthlessness of rent and tax collectors—great though these certainly were—probably did not damage Mediterranean populations as much as the recurrent outbreaks of disease for, as usual, disease found fresh scope in the wake of marching armies and fleeing populations. . . . The importance of disease in the entire process has long been recognized by historians; but because they have not been aware of the unusual force of a fresh infection arriving amid a population lacking any sort of established immunities or resistances, they have systematically underestimated the significance of the two initial epidemics triggering the entire devolution. There is, however, ample historical evidence of the catastrophic nature of epidemic invasions of virgin populations.

William H. McNeill, *Plagues and Peoples*. Garden City, NY: Anchor/Doubleday, 1976, pp. 106–107.

Unquestionably, by the third century Rome was increasingly losing the power, influence, and image that characterized its golden age during the previous two centuries. Largely to blame were the losses in population following the Antonine and Cyprian plagues, losses so high that they significantly exceeded the

Constantine's decision to move his empire's capital from Rome to Constantinople (pictured) represented one of many efforts to recover from decades of war and disease. These efforts eventually proved futile.

deaths and debilitating injuries resulting from all military engagements during the same period. Reforms initiated by the emperors Diocletian (284–305) and Constantine (306–337) aimed at increasing governmental efficiency, rebuilding the army, and bolstering the faltering economy provided only temporary relief. The most far-reaching imperial action came in 323, when the emperor Constantine decided to establish a second seat of government in the East in the well-fortified ancient Greek city of Byzantium. The residents renamed the city Constantinople to honor their emperor, and in 330 Constantine himself moved the capital of the empire from Rome to Constantinople. Later in the century, in 383, the emperor Theodosius I (379–395) officially divided the empire into Western and Eastern regions that, upon his death, essentially were governed as two separate empires.

The Eastern Roman Empire managed to maintain its power and territorial integrity. This was largely due to its well-fortified capital city, Constantinople; its exceptional army and navy; and, for the most part, its adept leadership. The Western Roman Empire, on the other hand, ultimately proved unable to defend itself. Little by little it was disassembled piecemeal by barbarian peoples either just migrating through Roman territory or marauding tribes intent upon establishing their own kingdoms in the wake of their destructive attacks. In 406 the Vandals and Alans invaded France from the north. In 409 the Vandals invaded Spain. In 410 the Visigoths sacked the city of Rome itself, forcing the Western emperor, Honorius (395–423), to withdraw his legions from England and station them on continental Europe. In 439 much of North Africa was lost to the Vandals. And in 452 the Huns, a nomadic Mongolian tribe under the leadership of the infamous Attila, invaded Italy. In 476 the final blow was dealt to the Western Roman Empire when Odoacer, a Germanic mercenary officer in the service of the Roman army, declared himself king of Italy and deposed Romulus Augustulus, the last of the Roman emperors in the West.

A half century later, however, with the accession of Justinian I (527–565) to the throne in Constantinople, it appeared that the

Western Roman Empire would be resurrected. Supported by his influential and powerful wife, Theodora, and by one of history's most outstanding and successful military leaders, Belisarius, Justinian set out early in his reign to reunite the empire by attempting to conquer and bring the western Mediterranean under his rule. By 541 he had succeeded in retaking a large portion of the former Roman Empire, including Italy, Dalmatia, North Africa, and southern Spain. With the extraordinary General Belisarius leading one of history's most proficient and resourceful armies, Justinian appeared to be well on the path to realizing his aspirations when a plague struck Constantinople. Once again, the dream of empire was transformed into a recurring nightmare when a new contagion began spreading throughout the *entire* Mediterranean world. According to author Kohn, Justinian himself contracted the disease and "though he recovered, his imperial ambitions did not. The mortality and disruption caused by [this most recent] plague prevented him from recapturing [all] the western provinces and restoring the former extent of the Roman Empire."[25] The grandeur that historians refer to when writing of ancient Rome was no more nor would it ever again become a reality.

CHAPTER THREE

Plague and the End of the Middle Ages

The traditional date for the fall of Rome is 476, the year the barbarian Odoacer dethroned the emperor of the West, Romulus Augustulus. But in reality, the final chapter of the decline and fall of the Roman Empire began during the reign of Justinian and was completed within fifty years of his death. Unquestionably, Justinian's armies succeeded in restoring much of the western Mediterranean to Roman rule. But the emperor's achievement was short-lived. For centuries historians attributed the eventual failure of Justinian's plan to reunite the Western and Eastern empires to the high cost of his imperial ambition: to achieve his ends he overextended his resources and was bankrupting the imperial treasury. Many historians now are of the opinion that the plague that struck Justinian's realm in 542 was far more virulent and momentous than originally had been presumed and was perhaps the primary reason his attempt at conquest ultimately failed. Historian and author William Rosen asserts that "the Plague of Justinian . . . killed at least twenty-five million people; depopulated entire cities; and depressed birth rates for generations precisely at the time that Justinian's armies had returned [nearly] the entire western Mediterranean to imperial control."[26] Historian William H. McNeill notes how visions of a reunited empire all but disappeared with the onset of the plague. He writes that "indeed, the failure of Justinian's efforts to restore imperial unity to the Mediterranean can be attributed in good part to the diminution of imperial resources stemming from the plague."[27]

Vivid Descriptions from Ancient Sources

Contemporary sources for the plague are both enlightening and consistent in their descriptions of its symptoms and severity. According to one such source, sixth-century Syrian lawyer Evagrius Scholasticus, the plague originated in Ethiopia, from where it "made a circuit of the whole world in succession, leaving, as I suppose, no part of the human race unvisited by the disease." He continues by noting that he was a victim and "was seized with what are termed buboes, while still a school-boy" and that he later "lost by its recurrence at different times several of my children, my wife, and many of my kin, as well of my domestic and country servants."[28] Procopius of Caesarea (a city in ancient Palestine), a sixth-century historian who accompanied General Belisarius during his battles in the West, offered the following description of the disease in his *Wars of Justinian*:

> [Victims] had a sudden fever, [though] the body showed no change from its previous color, nor was it hot as might be expected, but of such a [sluggish] sort that neither the sick themselves nor a physician who touched them could afford any suspicion of danger. . . . But on the same day in some cases, the next day in others, and in the rest not many days later, a bubonic swelling developed, and this took place not only in the groin, but also inside the armpits, and in some cases also beside the ears, and at different points on the thighs. . . . There ensued with some a deep coma, with others a violent delirium. . . . [They] suffered from insomnia and were victims of a distorted imagination. . . . And in those cases where neither coma nor delirium came on, the bubonic swelling became mortified and the sufferer, no longer able to endure the pain, died.[29]

Further on in his history, Procopius continues his account of the plague: "Some [victims] died at once; others after many days; and the bodies of some broke out with black blisters the size of a lentil. These did not live after one day, but died at once; and many were quickly killed by a vomiting of blood which attacked them. Physicians could not tell which cases were light and which severe and no remedies availed."[30]

Bubonic Plague

It was not until the eighth century that the plague eventually waned. Yet unlike most epidemics of the past, descriptions of its effects upon its victims by contemporary authors leave little doubt as to its diagnosis. The symptoms and bodily markings these writers describe unmistakably reveal the nature and identification of the plague. The swelling and appearance of buboes in the groin and armpits as well as other signs listed by Procopius and Evagrius Scholasticus indicate the presence of *Yersinia pestis* (formerly *Pasteurella pestis*), the bacterium responsible for bubonic plague. (The fifteenth edition of *Taber's Cyclopedic Medical Dictionary* notes that the term *plague* was "once used to describe any widespread contagious disease associated with a high death rate . . . [but is] now applied specifically to the highly fatal disease caused by Yersinia pestis.")

Bubonic plague is a zoonotic disease—that is, a disease that can be passed between animals and humans. Zoonotic diseases are common. It is estimated that slightly more than half of *all* humanity's infectious diseases are developed through contact with different animals. The plague itself is caused by a form of bacteria called a bacillus, a rod-shaped microbe. The bacillus was named *Yersinia pestis* (*Y. pestis*) after Alexandre Yersin, a Swiss bacteriologist who identified the organism during a bubonic plague outbreak in Hong Kong in 1894.

Black rats (*Rattus rattus*, also referred to as ship rats and common house rats) infected with *Y. pestis* are most frequently accountable for the introduction of plague to an area. Rats, however, are not directly responsible for infecting humans. Rather, the bacteria are passed from rats to humans through a vector, or carrier, the common Oriental rat flea. The process is relatively straightforward. A flea will instinctively alight on a rat. If the rat is infected, the flea itself will become infected when it bites the rodent and sucks in its bacteria-laden blood. When the rat comes in contact with humans, the flea typically will move on to a human host. By this time, the colonies of *Y. pestis* within the flea

Ancient writers describe the terrible appearance of bubonic plague at various times in history. The disease was marked by the growth of dark, painful blisters called buboes. Delirium and death usually followed.

have likely multiplied to the point where the flea's digestive track is blocked off due to the accumulation of bacteria. Consequently, when the flea bites its human host, it regurgitates the bacteria into the host's circulatory system, thereby infecting its victim.

The Three Forms of Plague

Plague can occur in three forms. The first and most common type is bubonic. Signs of the bubonic variety will generally surface two to six days after *Y. pestis* has entered the body. The victim will be assailed by multiple symptoms, including fever, bodily weakness, chills, and headaches. Lymph nodes, usually in the groin and armpits, will enlarge (that is, form buboes) and grow progressively painful due to increasing inflammation. Eventually the buboes become necrotic (the tissue dies and blackens) and begin to suppurate (release foul-smelling pus). Within three to five days, the infection will spread to the kidneys, liver, and, at times, the meninges (connective tissue layers) of the brain. Once the infection reaches this point, death is virtually certain. The mortality rate of untreated cases of bubonic plague can range from 60 percent to as high as 90 percent.

Septicemic plague, the second variety, occurs when *Y. pestis* invades the bloodstream directly. Symptoms of the blood infection include feelings of exhaustion, fever, and vomiting of blood. If the numbers of bacilli are great enough and the resistance of the patient is low, the victim frequently will die before the disease has affected the lymph nodes or lungs. The death rate without treatment falls between 90 and 100 percent.

The third type is pneumonic plague. It is far more contagious than bubonic and septicemic since it is spread from person to person through inhalation of airborne bacilli. The primary site of infection is the lungs. Within one or two days of becoming infected, the victim gets an intense reaction in the lungs, including a massive infiltration of fluids, severe hemorrhaging, and an almost nonstop oozing of watery, blood-laced expectorant. Within a few hours of the onset of these symptoms, body temperatures will rise to 103° to 104 °F (39° to 40 °C), tachycardia (racing heartbeat) will occur, and the victim will become delirious. Without antibiotic therapy, virtually all individuals infected will die within seventy-two hours. Of the three, pneumonic is the deadliest and rarest form of plague.

Although the Mediterranean world was free of plague from the eighth century, the inhabitants of Europe were never completely free from disease or pestilence of one kind or another. Indeed, persons living in both cities and countryside suffered from the nearly perpetual presence of a different kind of epidemic—filth and poverty. In her book *Deadly Companions*, Dorothy H. Crawford depicts the appalling nature and degree of the situation:

> In medieval Europe virtually everyone was infested with blood-sucking parasites and their homes were colonized by equally infested mice and rats. Most people in farming villages lived along with their livestock in tiny single-storey, thatched hovels which were dark, cramped and airless. As the population expanded and small communities grew into towns, the situation got steadily worse. With no facilities for waste disposal everything was thrown out into the narrow lanes that ran between the dwellings so that these dark, dank conduits became quagmires of mud, human and animal excreta and garbage, most of which ended up in the rivers that served as the water supply. In these unhygienic surroundings it is no wonder that microbes flourished . . . and lack of personal hygiene allow vectors like fleas and lice to prosper.[31]

A Rise in Population

Such dismal and unsanitary living conditions largely explain why epidemics of any sort occurred and flourished in Europe during the Middle Ages along with an abundance of common illnesses

The Justinian Plague

The Justinian Plague lasted too long and the mortality rate was too high to allow the emperor and his successors to restore or even hold a large part of Rome's western territories. Microbiologist Dorothy H. Crawford outlines the extent of the plague in both time lasted and lives taken.

> After the centuries of strife, the Emperor Justinian managed briefly to reconquer North Africa, Italy and Spain, and to reunite the Roman Empire in the sixth century AD, but when plague struck Constantinople it heralded a series of epidemic cycles that lasted for two centuries. It marked the end of the empire, the relative isolation of Europe in the West and the expansion of Islam in the East. In Constantinople the Justinian plague lasted for a year, killing a quarter of the population—10,000 people a day at its height. Justinian himself survived an attack, but as the epidemic surged both East and West throughout the empire it left few in its wake to perform essential tasks and the emperor was powerless to protect the newly united territories. The overall death toll in the two empires [East and West] is estimated at 100 million.

Dorothy H. Crawford, *Deadly Companions*. Oxford, UK: Oxford University Press, 2007, p. 79.

such as colds, fevers, and skin and digestive disorders. But what is noteworthy, if not surprising, is that despite the lack of sanitation, a dramatic increase in population occurred during the High Middle Ages from the eleventh to the fourteenth centuries. While demographic figures vary, the rise in the total numbers of people in Europe seems to have increased somewhere between 300 to 400 percent or from 30 million to 120 million. Historians have

Medieval European cities (such as the one depicted here) were dark, cramped, and airless. Given these dismal and unsanitary living conditions, illnesses flourished.

offered several explanations for this striking rise in population. Included among them are favorable climate changes, the absence of epidemics and foreign invaders, and an increase in the number of rural farming communities. The latter resulted from a widespread policy among the nobility of providing rewards to peasants in return for their cooperation in converting swamps and forests owned by the nobles into productive agricultural land.

But by far, it was the surprising and enormous increase in agricultural production that provided a foundation for a parallel rise in the birthrate throughout most of Europe. (History verifies that the availability and abundance of food almost invariably leads to population growth.) The increase in food was hastened by a series of technological innovations occurring in combination with the expanded use of certain farming techniques, many of which were novel to Europe. The advances were numerous and included the use of horses in place of oxen as beasts of burden. Along with horses came the horse collar and the heavy plow mounted on wheels, both of which made it possible to significantly increase the amount of land plowed and to reach the deeper soil where larger amounts of rich nutrients lie buried after endless decades of organic decay. All of this created for peasant farmers the advantage of being able to rotate their crops annually over three fields instead of two, thereby freeing up additional fields to be planted each year. And probably the most striking innovation was the introduction of the windmill, which harnessed the power of wind in areas where there were no streams and where rainfall was minimal. Since European society was primarily agrarian, medieval historians typically refer to this specific period during the Middle Ages as a time of economic revival.

The Plague Returns

Relative prosperity, however, does not render a population immune to disease and in some cases can even be a contributing factor. For one thing, population increases accelerate the growth in size of cities, towns, and rural villages. This fosters crowded and unsanitary living conditions, which in turn create an environment favorable to the contracting and spread of epidemics. Concurrently, increases in wealth and human numbers encourage and support an expansion of foreign trade where disease-causing microbes can be transported to unsuspecting and potentially vulnerable cities. And so it was in the fourteenth century during the so-called economic revival that conditions were evolving that would once again make possible the deadly specter of bubonic plague throughout Europe and much of the rest of the world. Significantly, the second plague would ultimately prove far, far more disastrous than the first.

The plague began in central Asia in the early 1330s. It moved westward and during its trek claimed an estimated 25 million Asiatic lives, mostly Chinese and Indians. In 1347 it entered the Byzantine capital of Constantinople and spread from there via cargo ships to the western Mediterranean. The first cities infected were the port cities of Naples and Genoa in Italy and Marseille in France. The following year it began moving rapidly through most of western Europe and into large parts of North Africa. By 1349 the plague had laid claim to virtually all of Europe, North Africa, and the Middle East.

One of the most reliable and famous eyewitness accounts of the Black Death of 1347—so-called because of the black spots that appeared on the skin of its victims—was by Giovanni Boccaccio (1313–1375), a brilliant Italian poet, storyteller, and humanist. Boccaccio depicts the plague in his celebrated work *The Decameron*, a collection of one hundred short stories narrated by a fictional group of ten Florentines who fled the city of Florence at the peak of the epidemic. It is in the introduction of *The Decameron* that Boccaccio presents his vivid and despairing account of the terrible toll the disease had exacted on his beloved city.

Boccaccio describes the initial symptoms, namely the characteristic swellings, or buboes, under the armpit or in the groin. As the disease progressed, black or dark blue spots would appear on the skin and eventually over the entire body. The spots would be a sign of approaching death. He then notes that the advice or remedies concocted by physicians were all useless and that once the buboes or black spots appeared, nearly all victims died within three days of the onset of symptoms. While many sought solace in solemn prayer, others, facing what they believed to be inevitable death, chose to spend their final days engaged in blatant debauchery. The law was of little use since, as Boccaccio notes, "the authority of the laws, both human and divine, was destroyed through the death of the lawful ministers and officers. For they all

Rotting Corpses and Silent Bells

Historian Mary Dobson describes the heart-wrenching human toll wrought by the plague. The unbelievable nature and effect of the epidemic is captured in the words of the Italian poet Petrarch as he laments the passing of his one true love, Laura.

> Everywhere—from the China Sea to the Mediterranean, across vast swathes of continental Europe and the British Isles, to the northern reaches of Scandinavia and Russia—countless [plague victims] were buried by surviving family and friends, tossed onto rattling carts, buried in pest pits, or left to rot in the midday sun, to be devoured by wolves, pigs and dogs. In Venice the dead were dropped into gondolas and rowed out to sea with cries of *"Corpi morti, corpi morti"* ["dead bodies, dead bodies"]. The smell of death was all-pervading—in the fetid breath and buboes of the afflicted, in the filthy alleys of crowded towns and villages, in the ghost ships crewed by dying sailors, in the mass graves stacked high with putrefying corpses. . . . With sadness and stenches came a dreadful silence. In some places even the funeral bells and weeping ceased—for *"all expected to die."* Petrarch [the Italian poet], who had lost his beloved Laura to the plague in Avignon in 1348, noted the vast and dreadful silence hovering over the world. *"Is it possible,"* he wondered, *"that posterity can believe these things? For we, who have seen them, can hardly believe them."*

Mary Dobson, *Disease: The Extraordinary Stories Behind History's Deadliest Killers.* London: Quercus, 2007, p. 14.

died, or lay so sick or in want of servants and attendants, that they could not carry out any duty. Hence everyone did as he pleased."[32]

Boccaccio continued his account, noting that once someone contracted the plague, he or she would often be ignored and even abandoned by neighbors, friends, and family. "The terror of the time," he wrote, "so afflicted the hearts of men that brother forsook brother, uncle abandoned nephew, and wife left husband. Incredible as it seems, fathers and mothers fled away from their own children." Perhaps most telling of all, there was little or no ceremony accompanying the burial of the dead. Boccaccio recounts the lack of care and compassion displayed at burial processions:

> Very few would accompany the body to the grave, not even the neighbors, even though the deceased had been an honorable citizen. Only the meanest [lowest] kind of people, gravediggers, coffin-bearers, and the like, who served only for money, made up the procession. The coffin being mounted on their shoulders, they would run with it hastily to the nearest church with four or six poor priests following, sometimes without lights, and, a short service being said, the body would be irreverently thrown into the first open grave they found.[33]

Twenty-Five Million More Deaths

This second recurrence of bubonic plague (1347–1352) ran its course in five years and claimed at least 25 million lives in Europe alone. (In some areas, the mortality rate ran as high as 75 percent of the population.) Ironically, these high figures did not negatively influence the continent's economy to any obvious extent. When the plague struck, the population of Europe was at its highest peak ever. Consequently, there were sufficient agricultural and nonagricultural workers to fill most of the worker vacancies created by the plague. However, the issue of worker shortages would eventually come to dominate the socioeconomic landscape since the plague of 1347 was only the first of nearly twenty more outbreaks that continued to ravage Europe intermittently for the next three hundred years. While some occurrences remained local and passed in a year, others were widespread and lingered up to fifteen years.

Bubonic plague unleashed its final major assault upon Europe in 1665 through 1666. Referred to as the Great Plague of London, it was thoroughly documented in *A Journal of the Plague Year*, a work authored by the famous diarist Samuel Pepys. A naval administrator for the English government and a member of Parliament, Pepys remained in London during the plague to record its devastation. In August 1665 he entered into his diary the following comment, which focuses upon the alarming increase in the death toll in the capital city: "In the city died this week 7,496, and of them 6,102 of the plague. But it is feared that the true number of the dead this week is near 10,000; partly from the poor who cannot be taken notice of, through the greatness of the number, and partly from the Quakers and others that will not have any bells rung for them."[34] Most historians estimate that 100,000 persons (nearly a quarter of the population) died in London as a result of the Great Plague. The numbers would have been higher were it not for the so-called Great Fire of London, which broke out on September 2, 1666. The fire began at a baker's shop on Pudding Lane in central London and raged for four days, destroying nearly 80 percent of the city. Fortunately, it also destroyed many rats and fleas who were carriers of the plague bacillus.

A Catastrophe Without Parallel

Although there have been several waves of bubonic plague throughout the world since the Middle Ages, none has equaled either the mortality rate or the economic and political impact of the pandemic that descended upon humanity during the fourteenth to seventeenth centuries. By the end of the fourteenth century, the population of Europe and the rest of the world had dropped from nearly half a billion to about 300 million. In fact, most historians would agree that the Black Death claimed more lives proportionate to the population of the affected areas than any other known epidemic or major war. In his book *Disease and History,* Frederick F. Cartwright asserts that "the Black Death was not just another

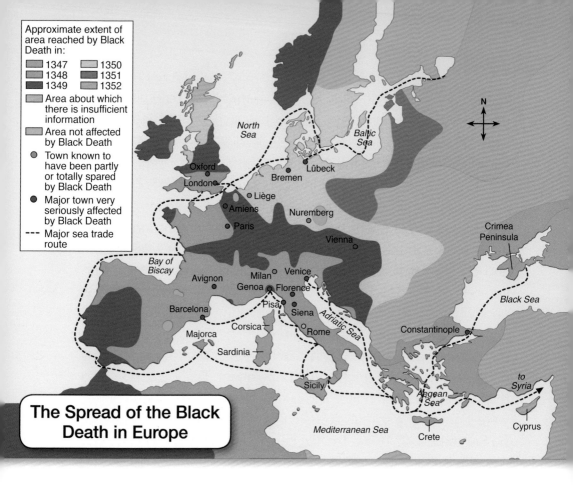

North
Sea

Baltic
Sea

N

Oxford
London
Liège
Amiens
Paris
Bremen
Lûbeck
Nuremberg
Vienna
Crimea
Peninsula

Bay of
Biscay

Avignon
Milan
Venice
Genoa
Florence
Pisa
Siena
Adriatic Sea
Rome
Barcelona
Majorca
Corsica
Sardinia
Sicily
Black Sea

Constantinople

to
Syria

Cyprus

Aegean
Sea

Crete

Mediterranean Sea

The Spread of the Black Death in Europe

incident in the long list of epidemics which have smitten the world. It was probably the greatest European catastrophe in history."[35]

The deaths of so many medieval laborers, both rural and urban, led to the ruin of a large majority of landowners. Without workers to sow their crops, there could be little or no harvests from which to derive their profits. The economic decline of the landlords would have a powerful and far-reaching effect upon society. Politically, it was the landowners who made up the feudal nobility, the ruling class of the medieval world. Their decrease in power and influence brought about a corresponding growth in the authority and strength of kings and the nations over which they ruled. The basis of political control now shifted away from the individual feudal estates in favor of the larger and more centralized national monarchies. It was this increase in royal dominance that ushered in the era of the modern nation-state.

As for the workers themselves, being in such short supply they had little difficulty peddling their labors to an emerging class of entrepreneurs. This combination of labor and business provided the nucleus of a new, expanding, and highly profitable system known as capitalism. George C. Kohn, the author of several historical reference books, wrote that "to many historians, the Black Death marked the end of the Middle Ages and the start of the modern age. Its devastation cleared the way for Europeans to begin to reorganize their societies, to systematize landholding relations between owner/farmer and tenant/laborer on the basis of rent, and to strike a balance between capital and labor."[36]

But what was destined to benefit humankind most at the dawn of this new age was a transformation in science and technology that was beginning to spread throughout Europe. Labeled the *Scientific Revolution* by historians, it was a defining moment in European and world history—an intellectually fertile period when several generations of creative thinkers began applying new methods of study to explore the mysteries of the physical and biological worlds. Critical thinking and objective experimentation started to replace superstition and the blind acceptance of outworn and unproven authority that had characterized most of the ancient and medieval schools of thought. Philosophers and scientists alike began viewing the earth and all that it held through a far wider prism. As they employed their new methods, previously unimaginable and unsolvable mysteries began revealing their secrets. More importantly, scientists and visionaries began applying much of what they discovered to new and useful purposes, all the while discarding antiquated doctrines and ideas that were deemed worthless and beyond redemption. This unique school of thought was leading humanity and the healing arts into a world never before known—a world where disease-bearing microbes were destined to become the victims and no longer the perpetrators.

CHAPTER FOUR

The Beginnings of Germ Theory

During the Greco-Roman and medieval periods, it was widely thought that miasma was one of the most frequent causes of sickness, especially epidemics such as cholera, bubonic plague, malaria, and other outbreaks comparable in nature. *Miasma* (derived from the Greek word for "pollution") was thought to be a particle-filled mist or vapor that carried within it poisonous impurities derived from rotting organic substances such as vegetables and animal and human flesh. Physicians and others readily endorsed the notion that infections were caused by deadly miasmatic fogs passing through field, village, and town. Lois N. Magner, historian and professor emerita, Purdue University, stresses how others looked to the heavens for answers, attributing plagues such as the Black Death to "a malign conjunction of Saturn, Jupiter, and Mars."[37] The conquest of disease was unlikely as long as society continued to subscribe to irrational beliefs such as these. The potential for cure and prevention of disease would remain all but impossible until doctors recognized the existence and responsibility of transmittable microorganisms. In other words, medical progress in the area of infectious diseases ultimately awaited a single, fundamental realization: epidemics, pandemics, and any other incidents of infection all result from a successful invasion of the human body by germs.

Living Microorganisms

One of the first scientists ever to propose a germ theory of disease was the Italian physician Girolamo Fracastoro (c. 1478–1553). Born in Verona, Italy, he taught medicine at the University of Padua and is probably best known for describing and naming the venereal disease syphilis. After an extensive study of epidemic diseases, he determined that diseases were caused not by dead, decaying matter found in miasma but by living, minute organisms. Moreover, he believed these microbes differed in size and shape and that each individually was responsible for a specific disease. He outlined his philosophy in *On Contagion and Contagious Diseases*, a work published in 1546. According to microbiologist Dorothy H. Crawford, Fracastoro theorized

> that epidemic diseases like smallpox and measles were caused by seminaria (seeds) which spread the contagion from one person to another. He envisaged these seeds spreading by three possible routes: direct contact, contamination of inanimate objects like clothes and blankets, or through the air. Fracastoro's seed[s] may not quite resemble living bacteria, but they are uncannily like viruses.[38]

A true visionary, Fracastoro anticipated the germ theory of infectious diseases by three centuries.

But it would take more than theories alone to penetrate the thick walls of ancient and medieval superstition, walls that had been reinforced by centuries of custom and practice. The simple fact was that in this new age of science, theories were only the starting point in the battle to conquer disease. This was especially true in the medical sciences, where observable and verifiable data would become the primary vehicles in the quest for accurate diagnoses and treatment of diseases.

A giant leap toward discovering the germ theory of disease took place in the seventeenth century in the town of Delft in the Netherlands. Antoni van Leeuwenhoek (1632–1723), a tradesman and later inspector of weights and measures for the town, took up a hobby that in time evolved into a near full-time occupation—the grinding of lenses to be used in microscopes. The development of microscopes had preceded Van Leeuwenhoek by nearly a century. But Van Leeuwenhoek's obsessive desire to explore a world until then inaccessible to the naked eye elevated what began as an amateur pastime to a degree of professional excellence never before achieved. His microscopes were capable of capturing that previously invisible world by magnifying objects ten to twenty times greater than all earlier ones. Moreover, Van Leeuwenhoek was the first scientist to publish pictorial representations of what he had discovered through the lenses of his microscopes. Referring to the microbes he observed as *animalcules* ("tiny animals"), he in time came to realize that they could be found virtually everywhere—in water, in air, in his neighbor's teeth, and in his own feces.

Van Leeuwenhoek's fame spread as a result of the more than four hundred publications in which he described and illustrated his microscopic observations. Indeed, his fame brought him personal visits from Peter the Great of Russia, James II of England, and Frederick II of Prussia. His work was also widely regarded by Europe's scientific community, as evidenced by his election into the prestigious Royal Society of England and the French Academy of Sciences. Nor were his achievements tarnished by the fact that he never even suspected that his animalcules played a role in human disease. As noted by John Simmons, a science biographer and a member of the New York Academy of Sciences, "Leeuwenhoek had no reason to suspect that microbes such as found in his neighbor's teeth could cause disease, because his neighbor was healthy. But perhaps a better answer is that the germ theory of disease required a chemistry which was not coherently formulated for another century and a half."[39]

Cholera and Miasma Theory

Despite the fact that for nearly two centuries many of Europe's physicians and scientists were aware of the existence of microbes, the miasma theory of disease held on as the dominant school of thought well into the nineteenth century. The role played by bacteria, viruses, and other microscopic agents in promoting disease remained, for the most part, unproven and therefore not seriously considered. In 1849, however, an English physician, John Snow (1813–1858), published an essay entitled *On the Mode of Communication of Cholera*. In the essay, Snow clearly outlined the mechanism by which cholera was transmitted in drinking water. His conclusions were nearly a complete repudiation of miasma as a possible causative factor.

From his earliest days in medicine, Snow had questioned the essentials of miasma theory. While working in 1832 as a physician's apprentice in Newcastle, a mining town in northern England, the nineteen-year-old Snow witnessed an outbreak of cholera that the local medical establishment attributed to miasmic vapors. Convinced that the disease was not transmitted by air, he noted that "there are a number of facts that have been thought to oppose this evidence: numerous persons [have] intercourse [contact] with the sick without being affected, and a great number [contract] the disease who have no apparent connection with other patients." The precocious young apprentice then went on to study the digestive tract of some of the deceased victims of the outbreak, noting that there was a "local [infection] of the mucous membrane of the alimentary canal [the entire digestive tract from mouth to anus]." Based on his examination, he concluded that

> the disease must be something which passes from the mucous membrane of the alimentary canal of one patient to that of another, which it can only do by being swallowed; and as the disease grows in a community by what it feeds upon, attacking a few people in a town at first, and then becoming more prevalent, it is clear that the cholera poison must multiply itself by a kind of growth . . . this increase taking place in the alimentary canal.[40]

English physician John Snow discovered the source of a mid-1800s cholera outbreak in London to be a public water pump (similar to the one depicted here). Snow proved that cholera spreads by ingestion and not, as most people believed, through inhalation of toxic air particles.

Following an outbreak of cholera in 1854 in London's Soho district, Snow published a second article containing additional evidence in support of his theory that cholera spreads by ingestion, not by the inhalation of toxic air particles. He reached his conclusion after interviewing a large number of Soho residents. The interviews pointed him in the direction of the source of the infection—a water pump located on Broad Street in London that delivered water to residents of the district. Snow later created a dot map of the entire area hit by the epidemic and was able to illustrate that overwhelmingly, the largest number of cases occurred in homes supplied by the Broad Street pump.

Snow then discovered that several commercial water companies drew their water from the Thames River, where most of London's sewage was dumped. However, one particular company, Southwark and Vauxhall, drew its water downstream of the sewage deposits, thereby distributing water contaminated by the waste and refuse. Predictably, it was Southwark and Vauxhall that supplied its water through the Broad Street pump. Added studies revealed that the incidence of cholera in those areas of Soho whose drinking water came from downstream of the sewage was nine times greater than those sections whose water was taken upstream (before the water made contact with the sewage). It was through Snow's efforts that the Broad Street pump eventually was shut down, resulting in a dramatic drop in cholera cases in the area. However, after repeated attempts at microscopic and chemical examination of the water emitted by the Broad Street pump, John Snow was unable to uncover any specific examples of what he had once referred to as the cholera poison. The causative agent, a bacterium called *Vibrio cholerae* (sometimes called the comma bacillus because of its shape), completely eluded him.

Louis Pasteur and Germ Theory

Although there is no evidence that Snow and his studies on cholera contributed either directly or even indirectly to the formulation of a widely accepted germ theory of disease, Snow's professional life and work are indicative of the new turn and radical direction medical science was taking in the nineteenth century. In a major article about the history of medicine, *Encyclopaedia Britannica* makes an assertion with which most historians of medicine would surely agree: "The overarching medical advance of the 19th century, certainly the most spectacular, was the conclusive demonstration that certain diseases, as well as the infection of surgical wounds, were directly caused by minute living organisms. This discovery changed the whole face of pathology and effected a complete revolution in the practice of surgery."[41] More important, this so-called overarching medical advance gave rise to bacteriology, a field of science that deals with microscopic organisms and their relationship to medicine and industrial and agricultural production. Significantly, the individual honored by his peers and successors as perhaps the most notable of the medical researchers in this extraordinary and indispensable field of modern medicine is the French scientist Louis Pasteur. In his book *The 100*, which prioritizes the world's one hundred most influential people (Pasteur is placed eleventh), Michael H. Hart emphasizes that "it was Pasteur's vigorous championship of the germ theory, substantiated by his numerous experiments and demonstrations that were the principal factor in convincing the scientific community that the theory was correct."[42]

By most standards of measure, Pasteur stands side by side with Isaac Newton, Charles Darwin, and Albert Einstein as one of the most consequential scientists in history. His work laid the foundation for preventive medicine, a new era in medicine that has resulted in an extension in life expectancy far beyond anything previously experienced or even imagined. But of greater importance, the discoveries he made and treatment therapies he established provided the momentum for the eventual development of wonder drugs such as antibiotics and specific vaccines that would revolutionize and dominate the practice of medicine in the twentieth and twenty-first centuries, saving tens of millions from premature death.

Pasteurization and Beyond

Louis Pasteur was born December 27, 1822, in the city of Dole, France. He was the third of five children born to Jean-Joseph Pasteur and Jeanne Roqui. His father, a decorated soldier who had fought in the Napoleonic Wars (1803–1815), was a tanner. During his youth, Pasteur developed a passion for painting and labored long and hard to hone his skills. Although encouraged in

Louis Pasteur and Posterity

John Simmons has long been associated with the reference work *Current Biography* and has written frequently about Nobel laureates in science. In his compendium *The Scientific 100* he highlights several of Pasteur's major achievements. Simmons underscores his enormous regard for Pasteur by listing him as the fifth-most influential scientist who ever lived.

It is difficult to avoid the conclusion, already drawn during his lifetime, that [Pasteur] belongs with the greatest scientists of history. Trained in chemistry, Pasteur turned to practical problems of fermentation in vinegar, wine, and beer after early discoveries in crystallography. During the last and most important phase of his career, he studied the causes of infectious illnesses in humans and animals and developed vaccines against anthrax and rabies, spawning much successful research to combat a host of other diseases. Pasteur's exceptional capacity to draw solid theoretical conclusions from his ceaseless experiments led to sweeping innovations in medicine. In principle, they have saved millions of lives and led to profound changes in everyday life around the world. It should be no surprise that Pasteur became a figure of legendary renown in his own time, or that today, with more critical attitudes toward great figures in science, his accomplishments are being subjected to more intense scrutiny.

John Simmons, *The Scientific 100: A Ranking of the Most Influential Scientists, Past and Present*. Secaucus, NJ: Citadel, 1996, p. 28.

his artistic endeavors by his teachers, his father considered art a luxury that Louis could ill afford. Respectful of his father's feelings, Pasteur focused on science and in 1842 earned a bachelor of science degree from the Royal College of Besançon (near the Swiss border). He then transferred to the École Normale Supérieure in Paris, where he became a teaching assistant to Jean-Baptiste-André Dumas, one of France's most prominent chemists. In 1847 he was awarded a doctorate in sciences with specialties in both physics and chemistry. The following year Pasteur joined the faculty at the University of Strasbourg as a professor of chemistry. After beginning his tenure at the university, he met and married Marie Laurent, the daughter of the university's rector. It was also at Strasbourg that his reputation as a researcher and teacher of chemistry began to broaden in France and beyond. But what would prove to be the pivotal period in his life occurred soon after Pasteur was appointed professor of chemistry and dean of the science faulty at the University of Lille. It was at Lille that he began to seriously explore the existence and impact of germs upon all living things and also there that he revealed an unwavering resolve to control their harmful and often deadly effects.

Lille was an industrial town located on the Belgian border and the home of numerous wineries and breweries. Teaching in the science department at the university, Pasteur became aware of the difficulties many of the wine and beer manufacturers encountered in the fermentation of their products. (Fermentation is the process by which sugar is converted to alcohol.) It was Monsieur Bigot, the father of one of Pasteur's students, who turned to the chemist in the summer of 1856 seeking a solution to a major problem he was facing at his winery. During the fermentation of the beetroot that Bigot was using to make wine, an inexplicable spoilage occurred where lactic acid was produced instead of alcohol.

Up to that point in time, virtually all chemists accepted that fermentation was a chemical reaction — that is, a process where various organic products chemically react with each other to form distinctively different products. In the case of wine, yeast is combined with fruit (like grapes) or vegetables (like beetroot) to chemically convert the sugar in the fruit/vegetables to alcohol. Being a chemist, Pasteur was well acquainted with these traditional beliefs held by most chemists. Nonetheless, he entered Bigot's factory not only armed with a microscope but also with an open mind—both of which prepared him for most any possibility or discovery. Thus equipped, he soon uncovered the presence of bacteria in the spoiled wine, leading him to conclude that the production of alcohol was a biological process, not a chemical one as was previously believed. And as he delved deeper and deeper into the issue of spoilage, he determined much to his surprise that along with harmful microbes there were beneficial bacteria that played a positive role in the fermentation process. Historian Magner outlines Pasteur's discovery:

> [While at Lille], Pasteur discovered microorganisms and optically active products of fermentation. His . . . studies led him to the hypothesis that the fermentation process was dependent on living germs or ferments. Previous speculations about the role of yeasts in fermentation had been ridiculed by the most illustrious organic chemists of the period, who argued that fermentation was a purely chemical process and that microorganisms were the *product* rather than the *cause* of fermentation. Further experiments on a variety of fermentations led Pasteur to the conclusion that all fermentations are caused by specific, organized ferments. Moreover, Pasteur suggested that living ferments might be the cause of infectious diseases as well as fermentations.[43]

Having now experienced the complexities inherent in the manufacture of alcoholic beverages, Pasteur began devoting much of his time to isolating and identifying the different organisms associated with the fermentation process of France's beer and wine industries. Since wine was one of his nation's most profitable exports, and the spoilage of wine was plaguing the entire industry, in 1863 he was encouraged to continue his work by France's emperor, Napoléon III. In due course Pasteur discovered that heating beer and wine at relatively high temperatures for only a few minutes would eliminate the harmful bacteria they contained. Yeasts and organisms advantageous to the process could then be added to the sterilized liquid without fear of eventual spoilage or contamination. Having effectively saved his country's premiere industry from near collapse, Pasteur was virtually elevated to the status of a national hero. (The heating process is called *pasteurization* in honor of its inventor, Louis Pasteur. Today it is practiced worldwide and used mostly by the dairy and food industries. The pasteurization of milk, especially, has substantially helped maintain the health and well-being of billions annually.)

The Conquest of Germs

In the years following his breakthrough discovery at the Lille factory, Pasteur's reputation grew far beyond the borders of his native France. Despite suffering a stroke in 1868 (the first of several) that impaired his speech and affected his dexterity and ability to walk, he continued his work. His accomplishments ranged from saving France's silk industry by identifying and subsequently eliminating bacteria infecting the eggs of silkworms to identifying microorganisms responsible for infecting both humans and those animals that are an essential part of humanity's food chain. A champion of the germ theory of disease, Pasteur's tireless advocacy bore fruit as he is universally regarded as one of the scientists most responsible for its eventual acceptance in the canons of modern medicine.

Moreover, his creative mind coupled with his successful experiments and unusual ability to articulate his ideas with credibility and clarity resonated with others, many of whom would join him on medicine's honor roll of eminent researchers. British surgeon Joseph Lister, for example, learned of Pasteur's work in 1865. Being a surgeon, he was painfully aware of the fact that it was common for more than 50 percent of all surgical patients to develop fatal infections at the site of their surgical wounds. Lister deduced that airborne microbes successfully entering the wound during the surgical procedure most likely were the culprits. Utilizing that information, he pioneered antiseptic surgery by inventing a carbolic acid spray used to kill germs in the operating room. Magner remarks that Lister "always attributed his success to his appreciation of Pasteur's argument that the 'septic property of the atmosphere' was due to germs suspended in the air and deposited on surfaces."[44] Robert Koch, a German physician and researcher, and a man often referred to as "the father of bacteriology," carried Lister's efforts still further. He discovered that using steam to sterilize surgical instruments along with the carbolic acid spray would further reduce the risk of infecting surgical wounds.

British surgeon Joseph Lister directs the use of carbolic acid spray during a surgical procedure. Lister's antiseptic spray heightened the chances of survival for surgical patients by killing germs in operating rooms.

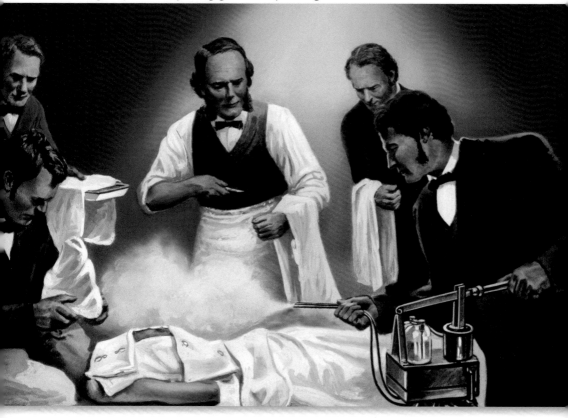

Robert Koch and Tuberculosis

Bacteriologist Robert Koch's efforts to isolate, identify, and eliminate the tubercle bacillus seemed nearly impossible. Yet he succeeded in his efforts and was eventually awarded a Nobel Prize in Medicine. Historian Lois N. Magner notes the difficulties facing Koch and the reasons why his success had such an enormous impact upon society.

> Of all the microbes studied by Koch, the tubercle bacillus was the most difficult to identify, isolate, and culture. On . . . [the] nutrient agar [a gel extracted from red algae and used in culture media], most bacteria produce large colonies within 2 days; the tubercle bacillus took 2 weeks to form visible colonies. In these investigations, superb microbiological technique, special media and staining techniques, and appropriate experimental animals were indispensable. But so too was the conviction that tuberculosis was a contagious bacterial disease, strong faith that the causative agent could be isolated, and almost infinite patience. The discovery of the tubercle bacillus and proof of its existence in diseased tissue swept away the confusion that had so long thwarted efforts to understand tuberculosis in all its many forms. . . . To understand the profound effect of Koch's announcement requires an appreciation of the ways in which this disease permeated the fabric of life in the nineteenth century. Tuberculosis was, in terms of the number of victims claimed, more devastating than the most dreaded epidemic diseases, including smallpox and cholera.

Lois N. Magner, *A History of Medicine*. New York: Marcel Dekker, 1992, p. 319.

The relationship between Pasteur and Koch, both the leading microbiologists of their day, was openly adversarial. There were several reasons for this. For one, the subject and nature of their respective projects and experiments occasionally overlapped, leading to the contentious issue of priority: Who should be credited with the discovery? Moreover, they had conflicting personalities. Pasteur tended to be outgoing with people and very transparent regarding his work, but Koch's public and professional persona was reserved and private. Lastly, both men were fervent nationalists. The second half of the nineteenth century was a period when their respective countries, France and Germany, were political adversaries that eventually went to war (Franco-Prussian War, 1870–1871).

Most historians would agree that Koch's contributions to medicine are enormous. Indeed, Koch's discoveries in the newly emerging field of bacteriology eventually earned him, in 1905, the Nobel Prize in Medicine for his work identifying the bacillus responsible for tuberculosis—*Mycobacterium tuberculosis*. Yet although Pasteur died six years before the Nobel Prize was first awarded, since 1908 eight Pasteur Institute scientists have received the Nobel Prize in Medicine. And among the majority of scientists and medical historians, Louis Pasteur is the acknowledged standard-bearer of what is arguably one of the most influential and productive eras in medicine.

Pasteur's Anthrax Vaccine

Perhaps Pasteur's most noteworthy and enduring accomplishments derive from his work on immunization. In 1879 an anthrax epidemic broke out in France and other parts of Europe, killing large numbers of sheep and infecting humans as well. Anthrax, an infectious disease caused by a rod-shaped bacterium, *Bacillus anthracis*, attacks both domestic and wild animals. With the patience and thoroughness that had always characterized his work, Pasteur isolated the causative bacillus and discovered that when

69

exposed to the air, it lost most of its virulence. (Like many others, *B. anthracis* is an anaerobic organism, meaning that it thrives in the absence of free oxygen. When exposed to oxygen, it weakens and eventually dies.) He then developed a vaccine made up of bacilli deliberately exposed to air and therefore considerably less potent. He administered the vaccine to twenty-five sheep and left a control group of twenty-five untreated. Two weeks after the inoculations were completed (Pasteur administered two inoculations twelve days apart), all of the sheep—vaccinated and unvaccinated—were administered a fully virulent strain of anthrax. As he had anticipated, the only sheep to die were those that were not vaccinated. According to science writer John Simmons, "These were controversial experiments which Pasteur had been challenged to perform. He carried them out with great flair, and they were widely reported in the press."[45]

Pasteur's success generated enthusiastic applause from the medical community for his bold and innovative approach to the killer anthrax. Although Edward Jenner, an English country doctor, had successfully developed a vaccine for smallpox nearly a century earlier, Jenner never fully understood the underlying principle that ensured the vaccine's success. Nor did he realize what was responsible for the disease itself, the variola virus. Pasteur, on the other hand, identified the organism involved (*B. anthracis*) and discovered a method with which to effectively weaken the organism (exposure to air). More importantly, he recognized that the immune systems of humans and animals are capable of building up immunity to a virulent organism when infected earlier by a carefully measured and weakened version of that organism. It was the weakened organism that Pasteur effectively utilized as the core of the vaccine itself.

The First Person Successfully Treated for Rabies

Louis Pasteur's worldwide prominence became decisively assured during the summer of 1885 when he successfully administered a

The French chemist Louis Pasteur oversees the vaccination of sheep during an 1879 anthrax epidemic that killed large numbers of sheep in France and other parts of Europe. Pasteur developed the vaccine after he successfully isolated the bacterium that causes the disease.

dramatic series of rabies vaccines to a nine-year-old Alsatian boy. The boy, Joseph Meister, was brought to Pasteur's laboratory by his mother on July 6, two days after being severely bitten by a rabid dog. Pasteur had begun working on the rabies problem three years earlier when he concluded that a microbe of some kind was responsible for the infection. Because the agent was a virus (considerably smaller in size than the average bacterium), he was unable to identify it and therefore found it necessary to employ entirely unique methods in his quest for an effective vaccine. He did recognize the lethality of the rabies microbe, however, and for that reason was hesitant to use it until he could first identify its precise nature. After seeing the Meister boy in his laboratory on that fateful day, his compassion for the badly mauled youth whispered that he set caution aside. Taking a sample of his most recently developed vaccine, he inoculated the young boy.

Several days later, on July 11, Pasteur wrote to his son-in-law, "All is going well. . . . The child sleeps well, has a good appetite, and the inoculated matter is absorbed into the system from one day to another without leaving a trace." But realizing that he would have to increase the virulence of the inoculations, Pasteur began to grow anxious. In a letter to his children, he wrote, "My dear children, your father has had another bad night; he is dreading the last inoculations on the child. And yet there can be no drawing back now! The boy continues in perfect health." After continuing the inoculations for several days, Pasteur sent the following message to his friend and biographer René Vallery-Radot:

My dear René, I think great things are coming to pass. Joseph Meister has just left the laboratory. The three last inoculations have left some pink marks under the skin, gradually widening and not at all tender. There is some action, which is becoming more intense as we approach the final inoculation, which will take place on Thursday, July 16. The lad is very well this morning, and has slept well, though slightly restless; he has a good appetite and no feverishness. . . . Perhaps one of the great medical facts of the century is going to take place; you would regret not having seen it![46]

The Dawn of a New Age in Medicine

Louis Pasteur's statement to his friend that "great things are coming to pass" was both timely and prophetic. For all but the last two centuries of human history, no effective treatments existed for *any* infectious diseases. Microbes freely had their way with the human race and many other living creatures, both great and small. Worse still, several of those microbes, like the rabies virus, were a pathway to almost certain death when contracted by a living host. Microbiologist Dorothy H. Crawford emphasizes that

> although through the ages many theories emerged to explain these phenomena [i.e., epidemics, individual infections], they were generally misguided, and the treatments they invoked usually did more harm than good. In fact right up until the eighteenth century most herbal remedies used by doctors, although they may on occasions have relieved suffering, contained no active ingredients; [and] the best advice a doctor could offer during epidemics was to flee or pray (or both).[47]

Yet because of the pioneering efforts of individuals like Van Leuwenhoek, Jenner, Snow, Lister, Koch, Pasteur, and countless others, humanity welcomed the twentieth century with a justifiable feeling of hope that the eventual elimination of all infectious diseases was surely achievable. Scientists like Pasteur and Koch demonstrated that although the process of finding a cure or preventive vaccine would frequently prove exceedingly challenging, the concept driving the process was relatively simple: identify the bacterium, virus, or other organism and then search until an effective way of treating it is found. Most of all, there was a growing conviction that with time and patience even the most virulent of conditions would eventually yield to some form of drug therapy.

CHAPTER FIVE

Will Infectious Diseases Be Conquered?

An unparalleled increase in the world's population validated the optimism handed down to the twentieth century by the eighteenth- and nineteenth-century pioneers in medicine. Six thousand years ago, when the first villages and cities appeared in the ancient Near East, the population of the world stood at approximately 8 million people. According to figures compiled by the US Census Bureau, by 1800 the number had risen to 900 million; it then more than doubled to over 2 billion by 1930 and reached 7.25 billion in 2015. Several factors have contributed to the substantial increases in the human population during the last two hundred years, including a rapid growth in agricultural output; technological innovations, such as sanitized human waste disposal and water filtration systems; recognizing the importance of educating the public in the essentials of personal hygiene; and the Industrial Revolution and other similar developments and events. But by far it was the discoveries and advances in medical science—driven primarily by the general acceptance of germ theory—that have had the most impact. More specifically, twentieth-century medicine's greatest successes have been in dealing with infectious diseases and can be credited to widespread vaccine use and antibiotic therapy. Both have been responsible for enhancing the physical well-being and longevity of human beings around the globe, most especially in the world's leading industrialized nations where the economic systems are strong and health care and educational systems are universal.

The Efficacy of Immunization

In the United States, for example, the Centers for Disease Control and Prevention (CDC), a government-funded agency, has recommended childhood immunization for as many as thirteen diseases. Included on the list are diphtheria, polio, smallpox, hepatitis A and B, pertussis (whooping cough), and tetanus. The CDC has reported dramatic declines in the morbidity rates (frequency with which a disease appears in a population) for diseases where the vaccination of children has been widely employed. Infections like smallpox, tetanus, and polio have experienced a nearly 100 percent decline in death rate in individuals who have been immunized. And of enormous consequence is the fact that vaccinations are administered globally (except where a political situation or reactionary government has been able to trump humanitarian considerations). Furthermore, immunization for the most part is not only safe but also relatively inexpensive, easy to dispense, and readily acceptable by peoples of nearly all ethnic and cultural backgrounds. However, it was the discovery of antibiotics that offered humanity what many believed was a category of drugs that eventually would prove capable of all but eradicating—along with vaccines—infectious diseases.

The era of antibiotic therapy is said to have begun in 1928 when a Scottish bacteriologist, Alexander Fleming, made a discovery that ultimately would revolutionize the practice of medicine. During World War I, Fleming, a captain in the Royal Army Medical Corps, worked in field hospitals treating wounded soldiers. He stood by helplessly watching as thousands of the young warriors died from infections that developed at the site of their wounds. Moved by his wartime experience, after returning to civilian life

A crowded street in the modern Indian city of Delhi is symbolic of a growing world population. Discoveries and advances in medical science, especially in dealing with infectious diseases, have contributed to unparalleled population growth.

he set up a laboratory at St. Mary's Hospital in London, where he experimented with agents that he hoped would kill or inhibit the growth of infectious bacteria in the human body. His early efforts yielded an occasional success, such as when he managed to isolate an enzyme, lysozyme, which the body's natural defenses release to fight off invading bacteria.

Penicillin Is Discovered

But it was on September 28, 1928, when Fleming entered his laboratory after a one-month holiday with his family, that medical history was to be made. Microbiologist Dorothy H. Crawford describes what the bacteriologist found waiting for him at St. Mary's on the historic day:

By all accounts Fleming was clever but forgetful and highly disorganized. His research laboratory at St Mary's Hospital . . . was always a mess. . . . [When he entered the laboratory that September day he found] some forgotten bacterial culture plates overrun with mould [mold], but as he was discarding them he noticed a clear zone round some fungal colonies [molds] where the bacterial growth was inhibited. Interested, he identified the mould as a new member of the *penicillium* family and set about extracting the antibacterial substance it produced. He called this "penicillin" and published his findings the following year.[48]

When he first figured out precisely what had happened and realized that his new find would transform the practice of medicine, Fleming decided to name his discovery *mold juice*. He later withdrew his original choice of name in favor of the more scientific *penicillin* after *Penicillium notatum*, the mold that produced it. Fleming's serendipitous finding proved to be the wonder drug of the twentieth century; in 1945 it earned its discoverer the Nobel Prize in Medicine.

The successful use of penicillin during World War II by military physicians was of considerable help in showcasing the drug before it attained worldwide distribution. Indeed, during the war doctors treating the wounded in field hospitals were able to successfully eliminate infections resulting from injuries obtained in battle. In their critically acclaimed book *The Killers Within*, authors Michael Shnayerson and Mark J. Plotkin note that military doctors were amazed to learn that "the new drug [penicillin] killed all the classic battlefield infections—gangrene, septicemia, and pneumonia—as well as a wide range of other infections: *Staphylococcus,* streptococci, tetanus-producing *Clostridium,* and the syphilis spirochete. Moreover, it had no toxic side effects other than an allergic reaction in rare cases."[49] The following anecdote offers ample evidence of the effectiveness of penicillin on the battlefield and the degree to which doctors were prepared to embrace it:

> Two years into the war the [US] Army issued its first meager supplies of penicillin, instructing physicians to use the precious drug sparingly, in doses of about 5,000 units (less than a third of what would be considered a minimal penicillin dose for minor infections in 1993). In those early days . . . such doses were capable of performing miracles, and the Army doctors were so impressed with the powers of penicillin that they collected the urine of patients who were on the drug and crystallized excreted penicillin for reuse on other GIs.[50]

With the astonishing effectiveness of the drug well established and pharmaceutical control agencies of various countries granting approval for its use, penicillin rapidly became the world's most prescribed medication for bacterial infections.

Penicillin is a type of antibiotic that is classified as bactericidal. It kills the bacterium directly by breaking down its cell wall and then interfering with the cell's normal functioning. Many other antibiotics are bacteriostatic—that is, they do not kill bacteria but prevent them from multiplying. (Viruses are not responsive to antibiotics.) In most cases the body's own defenses will ward off infection without outside help. For example, certain white blood cells called neutrophils play a leading role in preventing many harmful bacteria and viruses from establishing colonies in the body. This is accomplished through a process called phagocytosis, literally meaning "the process (osis) of eating up (phago) cells (cyt)." A neutrophil will literally stalk harmful microorganisms floating in the bloodstream. Eventually it will envelop the invader with its body as if swallowing it up and then kill the microbe by literally digesting it. Neutrophils will follow this same process when they encounter dead microorganisms in the bloodstream. But at times an individual's resistance is too low or the number and virulence of the invasive organisms are too high; without medical assistance, seri-

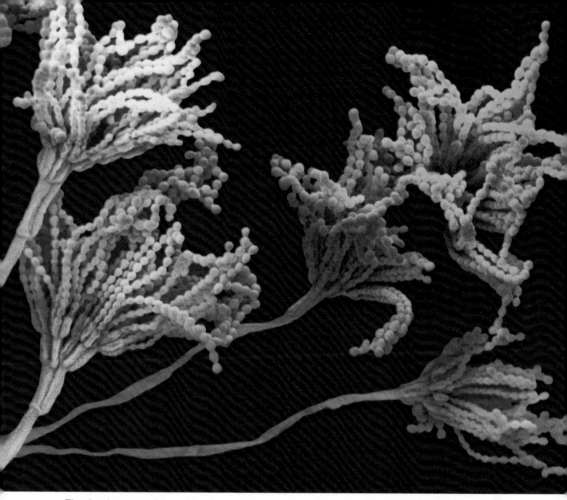

The development of the antibiotic penicillin grew from Alexander Fleming's experiments with Penicillium notatum *spores (pictured). Penicillin was first used on a widespread scale during World War II.*

ous bodily harm or even death may occur. It is at this juncture that antibiotics become necessary. It is also at this juncture that—prior to the advent of antibiotics—many patients would have died.

Additional Antibiotics

As is the case with penicillin, all antibiotics are naturally produced by molds and other living microorganisms, including bacteria themselves. Once the therapeutic value of Fleming's discovery became evident, it triggered an international search for additional antibiotics. Fleming himself noted that "the spectacular success of penicillin has stimulated the most intensive research into other antibiotics in the hope of finding something as good or even better."[51] During the 1940s and 1950s, others were developed, each capable of dealing with bacterial infections that were not readily responsive to penicillin. For example, tuberculosis was a leading cause of death worldwide in the first half of the twentieth century. The bacterium responsible for the disease is known as *Mycobacterium tuberculosis*. A rod-shaped microbe, it is also called Koch's bacillus, as it was first identified by Robert Koch in 1882. The tubercle bacillus was one such bacterium that was immune to penicillin therapy. Then, in August 1943, Albert Schatz, a twenty-three-year-old graduate student at Rutgers College of Agriculture in New Brunswick, New Jersey, discovered *Streptomyces griseus*, a powerful antibiotic produced not by a mold but by a bacterium inhabiting barnyard soil. Studies conducted on tuberculosis patients at the Mayo Clinic in Rochester, Minnesota, determined that the drug, given the name streptomycin, was successful in the treatment of the dreaded disease. (This quest for newer and more powerful antibiotics has continued and, of necessity, will continue. Thus far, well over 150 different antibiotics have been developed, approved, and are now being used.)

Because of the widespread use and lifesaving effect of antibiotics and immunizations, a significant rise in human life expectancy occurred during the twentieth century. Remarkably, the global rise in longevity between 1870 and 1970 literally doubled from thirty to sixty years, with the sharpest increases coming soon after World War II. Those advances in medicine that radically extended the life expectancy of people worldwide prompted many optimists to dare consider what previously was unimaginable: that humanity was on the threshold of virtually eliminating—or, at the very least, effectively controlling the spread of—all infectious diseases. William Bynum, emeritus professor for the history of medicine, University College London, refers to the period following the war as the "golden age of modern medicine." He notes that "doctors enjoyed an unprecedented era of prestige and trust. Infectious diseases were believed to be more or less conquered."[52]

A Premature Announcement

Even the US Department of Health, Education, and Welfare (HEW), after conferring with various medical specialists throughout the country, was quoted by Pulitzer Prize–winning science journalist Laurie Garrett as declaring that "man's mastery over nature has been vastly extended including his capacity to cope with diseases and other threats to human life and health."[53] Garrett also noted that William H. Stewart, US surgeon general from 1965 to 1969, echoed the enthusiasm of his HEW colleagues. Once, at a White House gathering of state health officers, he announced that infectious diseases were becoming a negligible problem thanks to medicine's extraordinary success in suppressing them; public funds could now be diverted from communicable to chronic diseases. Stewart most likely came to regret his words. After a lifetime as a distinguished pediatrician, epidemiologist, and US surgeon general, he unfortunately is best remembered as the public official who infamously once proclaimed: "It is time to close the book on infectious diseases, and declare the war against pestilence won."[54]

It was shortly after Stewart's widely publicized declaration that clinicians began noticing the emergence of new microbes, some of which were highly lethal. Crawford points out that

> since then they (i.e. the infectious microbes) have hit us at the rate of around one a year, and now the frequency is increasing, a scenario that seems to mirror events of 10,000 years ago when animal domestication prompted a spate of new human infections. And the reasons today are broadly the same as they were then—environmental changes that bring us into contact with "new" microbes which are then spread by travelers.[55]

An Increase in Zoonotic Diseases

Crawford's explanation for the "spate of new human infections" is supported by contemporary evidence. Historically, about 62 percent of all human pathogens were considered zoonotic (communicable from animals to humans). However, in 2015 the CDC noted that 75 percent of all recently emerging infectious diseases originated with animals, a significant percentage being foreign in origin. As the words *global village* imply, the inhabitants of Earth—human, nonhuman, and microbial—are now intimately interconnected by international transportation systems. This interconnection exists to a degree far beyond any previously known. Infectious diseases (zoonotic or otherwise), even those originating in remote parts of the world, can at any time be transmitted with the speed of an intercontinental airplane flight. Thus, diseases of foreign origin, combined with domestic health-related incidences, present formidable challenges to health care services not only in the United States but also throughout the world. Since 2013 the CDC has acknowledged more than 750 such health threats, a notable percentage being foreign in origin and most involving zoonotic diseases. In each case, scientists and doctors were called upon to respond; that is an average of just over one response per day.

Many of the new human infections are viral and therefore do not respond to antibiotic therapy. These include HIV (human immunodeficiency virus); Ebola, or hemorrhagic fever; SARS (severe acute respiratory syndrome); MERS (Middle East respiratory syndrome); avian influenza A; and many others. While some viruses have to date remained susceptible to immunization (smallpox, rabies, polio), most others have thus far proven unassailable. The reason most viruses seem to remain immune to vaccines and many other therapies is that the majority of them have fewer than ten genes. (Compare this to bacteria, which average about seven thousand genes, and humans, with approximately thirty thousand genes.) A mutation or change in the composition of just one viral gene could significantly alter the virus's virulence and power to infect. Viruses like HIV are known for their ability to mutate frequently even as they are being passed from carrier to carrier. Given that fact, the development of an effective vaccine at this point in time would be highly improbable.

Antibiotic-Resistant Bacteria

But the proliferation of viral and zoonotic diseases is only one of the medical issues facing the global village. The "spate of new human infections" includes a statistically significant number of bacterial infections that are antibiotic resistant. Ironically, the discoverer of penicillin, Alexander Fleming, was one of the first to warn the medical profession of the risks inherent in overmedicating with penicillin. In 1945, two years after the drug had reached the market, Fleming conducted a series of experiments from which he concluded that penicillin's arbitrary use would lead to resistance by the very bacteria it was supposed to eliminate. For example, certain varieties of *Staphylococcus aureus*, when exposed for great lengths of time to the drug, developed an enzyme that destroyed the penicillin before it could penetrate the bacterium's cell

Bacteria Have an Advantage

The twenty-first century has witnessed a substantial acceleration in the number of drug-resistant infectious microbes. Science writer Jessica Snyder Sachs, in her acclaimed book, *Good Germs, Bad Germs,* quotes microbiologist and Nobel laureate Joshua Lederberg as saying: "From an evolutionary point of view, the bacteria have always had the advantage. [They] can multiply and evolve a million times more rapidly than we can." Along with his wife, Esther, Lederberg revealed the mechanisms employed by bacteria to exchange genes and thereby transform their genetic structure enough to resist being killed off by existing antibiotics. Sachs herself then explained that bacteria "don't quibble about who belongs to what species when it come to swapping genes they need to thwart our antibiotics and, if it's in their interest, to wipe us out."

Quoted in Jessica Snyder Sachs, *Good Germs, Bad Germs: Health and Survival in a Bacterial World.* New York: Hill and Wang, 2007, p. 237.

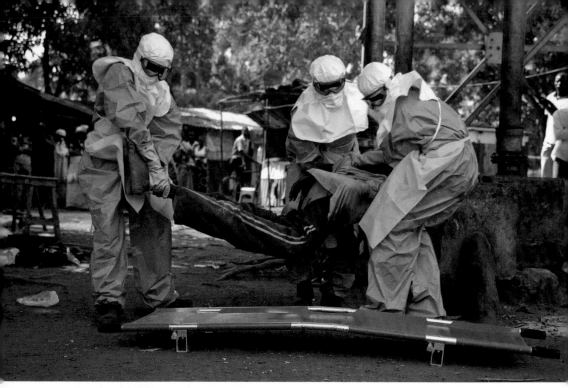

A suspected Ebola victim is removed from a town in the West African country of Guinea in 2015. Outbreaks of Ebola and other viral illnesses that do not respond to antibiotics are creating huge challenges for the world.

wall. Moreover, in an interview with the *New York Times,* Fleming pointed out that undermedicating also posed a serious threat. Critical of the indiscriminate use of low-dosage penicillin in many over-the-counter drugs, Fleming declared that "the greatest possibility of evil in self-medication is the use of too small doses so that instead of clearing up infection, the microbes are educated to resist penicillin. . . . [The penicillin-resistant bacteria will then reproduce and] be passed to other individuals and from them to others until they reach someone who gets septicemia or a pneumonia which penicillin cannot save."[56]

To cite an example, the British pharmaceutical giant Beecham and Bristol (now GlaxoSmithKline, the world's sixth-largest pharmaceutical company) developed a semisynthetic antibiotic, methicillin, for use against a staphylococcal pneumonia that patients were contracting while in hospitals. The staphylococcus was resistant to penicillin. The drug received worldwide publicity and acclaim in 1959 when an experimental dose was used to save the life of actress Elizabeth Taylor after she had been hospitalized while filming the epic movie *Cleopatra*. However, within five years European hospitals began warning of outbreaks of methicillin-resistant strains of *Staphylococcus aureus.* In her book *Good Germs, Bad Germs*, Jessica Snyder Sachs, a science writer and former managing editor of *Science Digest*, summarizes the situation with a quote from *Through the Looking-Glass*, Lewis Carroll's sequel to *Alice's Adventures in Wonderland*. The passage quoted was delivered by the Red Queen (one of the novel's characters). It is a fitting and clever metaphor for the problem that Alexander Fleming had warned of and the manufacturers of methicillin were facing: "Here, you see, it takes all the running you can do, to keep in the same place."[57] In other words, it appeared that bacteria, like humans, are capable of responding to existential dangers and that a new paradigm was being put in play. Whenever science developed a drug capable of eliminating or lessening the injurious effects of an infectious microbe, the bacteria involved would likely, in time, successfully develop a resistance to the drug.

Bacteria Become Resistant

In effect, that is precisely what was happening. The process works as follows: For a bacterium to successfully avoid being killed by an antibiotic like penicillin, it must possess a gene or several genes that are resistant to that specific drug. If a small number of bacteria possessing resistant genes are present in a large colony of *Staphylococcus aureus*, the use of penicillin would likely succeed in killing off *only* the bacteria without the resistant genes. The patient would be cured since the colony of infecting bacteria would now be greatly reduced and the patient's own immune system would be able to control the growth and virulence of the resistant bacteria. However, those surviving staphylococci that remained behind and were too few in number to cause an active infection in the patient were, nonetheless, being transferred from host to host during the course of casual contact among humans. At some point, the resistant staphylococci might enter the body of a new host (either by physical contact or inhalation) whose internal resistance was very low. In such a host, the staphylococci would eventually begin to reproduce at an exponential rate, and when the patient began to display symptoms of an infection, penicillin would be of little or no help. (Bacteria reproduce asexually by binary fission—namely, they split into two daughter cells, each of which is a replica of the original parent cell. The nature and ease of binary fission permits each organism to divide quickly and exponentially so that over a twenty-four-hour period, a single bacterium may be responsible for a billion offspring.)

Bacteria also engage in a form of "sex" that further helps explain their facility for developing resistance to antibiotics. The process is called *transformation* and occurs when, for no specific reason, two bacteria stick together and, in the process, transfer over a small part of their genetic material. If some of the genes transferred are drug resistant, the recipient of those genes will itself become resistant. In time, it will be responsible for the creation of its own drug-resistant colonies, and as long as potential hosts are available, successive generations of the bacteria will continue to reproduce until a new antibiotic is developed to eliminate them. What is interesting to note is that the Darwinian concept of "survival of the fittest" is obviously at play on the microscopic as well as the macroscopic level. When a bacterium is drug resistant, its survival chances are far greater than those less fit bacteria, which are susceptible to penicillin or other antibiotics.

Germ Warfare Past and Present

Finally, when considering the impact disease has had upon history and the ability of viruses and bacteria to mutate to unique stages of virulence, one should be mindful that the modern age is one of global terrorism; as such, the possibility of biological weapons (germ warfare) being put to use cannot be ignored. Historically, biological weapons have had many precedents. In 1347 the great walled city of Kaffa (now Feodosiya, Ukraine) was

Europe's Conquest of the New World: Germ Warfare?

Pulitzer Prize–winning author Jared Diamond exposes what might be construed as an unintentional example of germ warfare as well as an explanation for how a mere handful of Spanish soldiers managed to conquer an entire civilization. After centuries of exposure to the smallpox virus, the Spaniards—unwittingly—had developed immunity to the culprit. The Aztecs of the New World were not as fortunate.

> The importance of lethal microbes in human history is well illustrated by Europeans' conquest and depopulation of the New World. Far more Native Americans died in bed from Eurasian germs than on the battlefield from European guns and swords. Those germs undermined Indian resistance by killing most Indians and their leaders and by sapping the survivors' morale. For instance, in 1519 Cortés [Spanish military leader] landed on the coast of Mexico with 600 Spaniards, to conquer the fiercely militaristic Aztec Empire with a population of many millions. . . . What gave the Spaniards a decisive advantage was smallpox, which reached Mexico in 1520 with one infected slave arriving from Spanish Cuba. The resulting epidemic proceeded to kill nearly half of the Aztecs, including Emperor Cuitlahuac. Aztec survivors were demoralized by the mysterious illness that killed Indians and spared Spaniards, as if advertising the Spaniards' invincibility. By 1618, Mexico's initial population of about 20 million had plummeted to about 1.6 million.

Jared Diamond, *Guns, Germs, and Steel: The Fates of Human Societies*. New York: W.W. Norton, 1998, p. 210.

under siege by an army of Mongol warriors. A particularly virulent strain of plague had infected many of the Mongol soldiers. Unable to breach the walls of the city, the Mongols decided to catapult their infected corpses over the city walls, spreading the plague to the inhabitants of Kaffa. It is widely held by historians that Genoese cargo ships carrying goods from the Orient were anchored at Kaffa. During the catapulting episode, personnel onboard the ships contracted the plague and carried it to Constantinople, from where it was then transported throughout the western Mediterranean. More recently, Japan is alleged to have spread fleas infected with *Yersinia pestis* in some areas of China during World War II. And at the peak of the Cold War, both the United States and the Soviet Union developed (although never deployed) an aerosol technique for spreading the most lethal variety of plague, pneumonic plague.

Currently, the threat of biological weapons has ominous global implications. It is evident that germ warfare would be a particularly effective and efficient way to wreak havoc and death throughout an enemy's cities. Microbes would be easier to disguise and transport than explosive devices such as dynamite and atomic weapons. Moreover, if used in advance of an invasion, germs are capable of killing off large segments of the population without doing any damage to a city's essential infrastructure. Along with the weakened and demoralized survivors of the attack, intact roads, transportation centers, and communication buildings would be of enormous value to any successful invader. And it is conceivable that a sophisticated and scientifically adept adversary may one day possess the technology to genetically create microorganisms on a large scale that are resistant to all available immunizations and medications.

Of the nearly two hundred member states of the United Nations, it is believed that at least ten are engaged in the research of biological weapons at some level. Unlike the formidable technology involved in the manufacture of fissionable materials and nuclear weapons, the creation of biological weapons is quite easy to disguise during the research-and-development stage and relatively inexpensive to produce once ready for military use. Even small, economically backward countries and terrorist organizations could find ways to successfully embark upon germ warfare programs. Al Qaeda, for one, is known to have worked with the anthrax bacillus between 2001 and 2002 in laboratories located in Afghanistan before the United States and the Afghan Northern Alliance forced the terrorist group to abandon much of its territorial holdings in that country. Today many experts warn that a rogue nation or coalition of terrorists might one day possess the necessary competence and resolve to successfully unleash a biological weapon upon an unwary city anywhere in the world.

* * * * * *

Infectious diseases—whether let loose by nature, warfare, or any hidden means as yet to be revealed—have been a curse people of the world have had to endure. During the nineteenth century, scientific efforts to control and perhaps even eliminate this perennial scourge met with extraordinary success. Yet the sense of euphoria and achievement that existed within the international scientific community following the discoveries of men like Pasteur, Koch, Fleming, and Salk quickly evaporated as germs began demonstrating their resilience. Seemingly from nowhere, catastrophic viral infections like AIDS and Ebola began invading the human landscape. Other diseases, bacterial in nature, became totally resistant to traditional antibiotic therapy as the bacteria responsible for the infections underwent changes in genetic structure that rendered them immune.

Unless and until medical science uncovers methods of achieving complete control over the community of microscopic organisms that literally surrounds the human race, an effective

89

and lasting solution to the problem will remain beyond humanity's reach. And unless or until that happens, perhaps the words of British microbiologist and science journalist Bernard Dixon deserve an occasional thought. In his book *Power Unseen: How Microbes Rule the World*, Dixon writes:

> Consider the difference in size between some of the very tiniest and the very largest creatures on Earth. A small bacterium weighs as little as 0.00000000001 gram. A blue whale weighs about 100,000,000 grams. Yet a bacterium can kill a whale. . . . Such is the adaptability and versatility of microorganisms as compared with humans and other so-called "higher" organisms that they will doubtless continue to colonize and alter the face of the Earth long after we and the rest of our cohabitants have left the stage forever. Microbes, not macrobes, rule the world.[58]

SOURCE NOTES

Introduction: The Importance of Disease in History

1. Quoted in William McGuire and R.F.C. Hull, eds., *C.G. Jung Speaking: Interviews and Encounters.* Princeton, NJ: Princeton University Press, 1977, p. 248.
2. Will and Ariel Durant, *The Lessons of History.* New York: Simon & Schuster, 1968, p. 81.
3. Jared Diamond, *Guns, Germs, and Steel: The Fates of Human Societies.* New York: W.W. Norton, 1998, pp. 196–97.

Chapter One: Do Infectious Diseases Impact upon History?

4. Dorothy H. Crawford, *Deadly Companions: How Microbes Shaped Our History.* Oxford, UK: Oxford University Press, 2007, p. 75.
5. Paul Harvey, ed., *The Oxford Companion to Classical Literature.* Oxford, UK: Oxford University Press, 1962, p. 429.
6. Will Durant, *The Life of Greece.* New York: Simon & Schuster, 1939, p. 441.
7. Frederick F. Cartwright, *Disease and History.* New York: New American Library, 1974, pp. 14–15.
8. Quoted in University of Maryland Medical Center, "Plague of Athens: Another Medical Mystery Solved at University of Maryland," January 1, 1999. http://umm.edu.
9. Quoted in University of Maryland Medical Center, "Plague of Athens."
10. Quoted in John Carey, ed., *Eyewitness to History.* Cambridge, MA: Harvard University Press, 1987, p. 1.
11. Quoted in Logan Clendening, ed., *Sourcebook of Medical History.* New York: Dover, 1960, p. 28.
12. Quoted in Jon E. Lewis, ed., *The Mammoth Book of Eye-Witness History.* New York: Carroll & Graf, 1998, pp. 8–9.

13. Quoted in Clendening, ed., *Sourcebook of Medical History*, pp. 30–31.
14. Crawford, *Deadly Companions*, p. 75.
15. Cartwright, *Disease and History*, p. 15.
16. Edward McNall Burns, *Western Civilizations: Their History and Their Culture,* 8th ed. New York: W.W. Norton, 1973, p. 128.
17. William H. McNeill, *Plagues and Peoples*. Garden City, NY: Anchor/Doubleday, 1976, p. 94.

Chapter Two: Plague and the Fall of the Roman Empire
18. Burns, *Western Civilizations,* p. 157.
19. McNeill, *Plagues and Peoples*, p. 103.
20. David Potter, *The Emperors of Rome.* New York: Metro, 2007, p. 94.
21. Crawford, *Deadly Companions*, p. 78.
22. Pontius the Deacon, "The Life and Passion of Cyprian, Bishop and Martyr," Christian Classics Ethereal Library. www.ccel.org/cce/schaff/anf05.iv.iii.html.
23. George C. Kohn, *Encyclopedia of Plague and Pestilence: From Ancient Times to the Present*. New York: Facts On File, 2008, p. 85.
24. Crawford, *Deadly Companions*, p. 79.
25. Kohn, *Encyclopedia of Plague and Pestilence*, p. 216.

Chapter Three: Plague and the End of the Middle Ages
26. William Rosen, *Justinian's Flea*. New York: Viking Penguin, 2007, p. 3.
27. McNeill, *Plagues and Peoples*, p. 113.
28. Quoted in Rosen, *Justinian's Flea*, p. 219.
29. Quoted in Rosen, *Justinian's Flea*, pp. 217–18.
30. Quoted in Hans Zinsser, *Rats, Lice, and History.* New York: Little, Brown, 1935, p. 108.
31. Crawford, *Deadly Companions*, p. 82.
32. Quoted in Bruno Leone, ed., *The Middle Ages*. San Diego: Greenhaven, 2002, p. 177.

33. Quoted in Leone, ed., *The Middle Ages,* pp. 178, 179.

34. Quoted in Crawford, *Deadly Companions,* p. 89.

35. Cartwright, *Disease and History,* p. 43.

36. Kohn, *Encyclopedia of Plague and Pestilence*, p. 33.

Chapter Four: The Beginnings of Germ Theory

37. Lois N. Magner, *A History of Medicine.* New York: Marcel Dekker, 1992, p. 114.

38. Crawford, *Deadly Companions*, p. 164.

39. John Simmons, *The Scientific 100: A Ranking of the Most Influential Scientists, Past and Present.* Secaucus, NJ: Citadel, 1996, p. 263.

40. Quoted in Crawford, *Deadly Companions,* p. 134.

41. *Encyclopaedia Britannica,* "History of Medicine." www.britannica.com.

42. Michael H. Hart, *The 100: A Ranking of the Most Influential Persons in History.* Secaucus, NJ: Citadel, 1996, p. 61.

43. Magner, *A History of Medicine,* p. 310.

44. Magner, *A History of Medicine,* p. 299.

45. Simmons, *The Scientific 100,* p. 31.

46. Quoted in Harlow Shapley, Samuel Rapport, and Helen Wright, eds., *A Treasury of Science.* New York: Harper & Brothers, 1954, p. 598.

47. Crawford, *Deadly Companions,* p. 161.

Chapter Five: Will Infectious Diseases Be Conquered?

48. Crawford, *Deadly Companions*, p. 180.

49. Michael Shnayerson and Mark J. Plotkin, *The Killers Within: The Deadly Rise of Drug-Resistant Bacteria.* New York: Little, Brown, 2002, p. 34.

50. Laurie Garrett, *The Coming Plague: Newly Emerging Diseases in a World Out of Balance.* New York: Penguin, 1994, p. 4.

51. Quoted in Shapley, Rapport, and Wright, eds., *A Treasury of Science,* p. 628.

52. William Bynum, *The History of Medicine: A Very Short Introduction*. Oxford, UK: Oxford University Press, 2008. Kindle edition.
53. Quoted in Garrett, *The Coming Plague,* p. 33.
54. Quoted in Garrett, *The Coming Plague,* p. 33.
55. Crawford, *Deadly Companions,* p. 184.
56. Quoted in Shnayerson and Plotkin, *The Killers Within,* p. 35.
57. Quoted in Jessica Snyder Sachs, *Good Germs, Bad Germs: Health and Survival in a Bacterial World*. New York: Hill and Wang, 2007, p. 110.
58. Quoted in Garrett, *The Coming Plague*, p. 411.

FOR FURTHER RESEARCH

Books

Christine Auchora-Walske, *Antibiotics*. Edina, MN: ABDO, 2013.

Bryn Barnard, *Outbreak! Plagues That Changed History*. New York: Crown, 2005.

William Bynum, *The History of Medicine: A Very Short Introduction*. Oxford, UK: Oxford University Press, 2008.

Frederick F. Cartwright, *Disease and History*. London: Thistle, 2014.

Dorothy H. Crawford, *Deadly Companions: How Microbes Shaped Our History.* Oxford, UK: Oxford University Press, 2007.

Stephen Currie, *The Black Death*. San Diego: ReferencePoint, 2014.

Mary Dobson, *Disease: The Extraordinary Stories Behind History's Deadliest Killers*. London: Quercus, 2007.

Jeanne Guillemin, *Biological Weapons: From the Invention of State-Sponsored Programs to Contemporary Bioterrorism*. New York: Columbia University Press, 2005.

George C. Kohn, *Encyclopedia of Plague and Pestilence: From Ancient Times to the Present*. New York: Facts On File, 2008.

Michael B.A. Oldstone, *Viruses, Plagues, and History: Past, Present, and Future.* Oxford, UK: Oxford University Press, 2010.

William Rosen, *Justinian's Flea*. New York: Viking Penguin, 2007.

Jessica Snyder Sachs, *Good Germs, Bad Germs: Health and Survival in a Bacterial World*. New York: Hill and Wang, 2007.

Linda Wasmer Smith, *Louis Pasteur: Genius Disease Fighter*. Berkeley Heights, NJ: Enslow, 2015.

Carl Zimmer, *A Planet of Viruses*. Chicago: University of Chicago Press, 2012.

Websites

Centers for Disease Control and Prevention (www.cdc.gov). The Centers for Disease Control and Prevention is the leading public health institute of the United States. Its laboratories work to identify actual and potential health threats to the nation and are active in aiding in the control and prevention of disease.

Contagion: Historical Views of Diseases and Epidemics (http://ocp.hul.harvard.edu/contagion/index.html). At this extensive website from Harvard University, visitors can learn about some of the infectious diseases and epidemics that have occurred throughout human history. Included in the collection are articles written at the time of the epidemics, descriptions of many infectious diseases, and biographies of many important people who contributed to the germ theory of disease.

Mayo Clinic (www.mayoclinic.org). The Mayo Clinic, based in Rochester, Minnesota, is a nonprofit medical practice and medical research group. Founded in 1889, it is the largest nonprofit medical group in the world, employing nearly four thousand physicians and scientists. Its website is a comprehensive source of information for students and the general public on infectious diseases of all varieties.

Pasteur Institute (www.pasteur.fr/en). The Pasteur Institute is a nonprofit private foundation dedicated to research contributing to advances in medicine and public health. It works in conjunction with the World Health Organization and numerous worldwide public research institutions.

Robert Koch Institute (www.rki.de/EN/Home/homepage_node.html). The Robert Koch Institute in Berlin, Germany, has an

English-language site where visitors can learn about its latest research into such varied topics as hygiene, diabetes, the Ebola virus, and the value of vaccines. Click on "The Institute" and "History" links to read about the scientific contributions of Robert Koch and the institute's origins.

Vaccines.gov (www.vaccines.gov). This website is managed by the US Department of Health and Human Services. It offers extensive information about currently available vaccines and their benefits, efficacy, and safety.

World Health Organization (www.who.int). This organization is the United Nations public health agency. It tracks contagious disease outbreaks throughout the world, aiding in the prevention and management of global epidemics. It is also a valuable source for local emergent diseases that could potentially expand to pandemic proportions.

INDEX

PICTURE CREDITS

ABOUT THE AUTHOR

Bruno Leone earned undergraduate and graduate degrees in history from Arizona State University and the University of Minnesota. He currently lectures for the Osher Foundation at San Diego State University. His academic awards include a National Defense Education Act Fellowship, Woodrow Wilson Fellowship, two National Science Foundation grants, and a National Endowment for the Humanities Fellowship. He has written on a number of topics, including education, science, and history, his most recent publication being a biography of Charles Darwin. He is also an accomplished pianist who has recorded several CDs.